To Alasdair
from Dad
Christmas 1976.

The Ramayana

The Ramayana

Adapted from the English Translation of
Hari Prasad Shastri
by

Elizabeth Seeger

With Illustrations by Gordon Laite

J. M. Dent & Sons Limited

First published in Great Britain 1975
Text © 1969 by Elizabeth Seeger
Illustrations © 1969 by Gordon Laite
All rights reserved.
Printed in Great Britain by
Biddles Ltd, Guildford, Surrey
and bound at the
Aldine Press, Letchworth, Herts,
for J. M. Dent & Sons Ltd,
Aldine House, Albemarle Street, London.
ISBN 0 460 05098 2

Table of Contents

Author's Introduction

The Ramáyana is one of the two great epic stories of India, the other being the tale of the Pándavas and Kúravas, which is the core of the vast cyclopedia that is the Mahabhárata. Whereas there is much added material, much digression and repetition in the latter book, the Ramáyana is a straight-forward, sequential, romantic tale, composed by one person, though others have added to it and elaborated it. It is a poem of 24,000 couplets, about a quarter as long as the Mahabhárata.

The events that form the story must have taken place in the early days of the Aryan occupation of northern India. For an unknown length of time it was told and retold, enlarged and embroidered, until it was composed in its present form by the sage Valmiki. Scholars believe that he lived during the fourth century B.C. and that the poem was not written down in Sanskrit until the end of the sixth century A.D. During the intervening centuries it was learned by heart, with the prodigious memories of men who cannot read or write, and recited by them in ever-increasing areas of the country, starting in the northeast and penetrating to the west and to the farthest south, just as the story itself starts close to the border of Nepal in the north and proceeds through the forests of central India to Ceylon and back again. In our Middle Ages, written versions of it appeared in the different vernaculars of India, notably that composed by Kamban in Tamil, as early as the ninth century, and the rhapsodic poem of Tulsi Das in Hindi, as late as the sixteenth. This latter, far shorter than the original, has been widely read in northern India from the time of its writing to the present day.

It is always tempting to speculate on the origins of great

legends. We cannot know how many centuries before Christ
Rama may have lived, the son of a chieftain of a small state,
in far more primitive circumstances than the splendor and
luxury described in the poem. Yet he and his brothers and
his wife, people indistinguishable in appearance and habits
from hundreds and thousands of others, were so imbued with
the high moral standards and spiritual aspirations that char-
acterize the earliest thought of the Aryans, that they have lived
for more than two millennia in the hearts and minds of a
great people, more vividly, perhaps, than in their own in-
discoverable lifetimes. It is heartening, too, at the present time,
when moral and spiritual values are largely disregarded and
scoffed at, to realize that virtue and nobility are cherished
beyond all things and held fast in the hearts of men, both in
the East and in the West.

The monkeys, who also form such an important and lovable
part of the story, are supposed by scholars to have been a
friendly tribe of people who inhabited the enormous forests of
central India, far less civilized than the Aryans, still fighting
with clubs and stones, not yet using the bow and arrow. And
the demons were probably an alien race, established on Ceylon
and beginning to invade the southern mainland, who were
more civilized but more savage than the forest tribes. It would
be a mistake, however, for the storyteller to take the historical
point of view and to deny the monkeys their tails and the
demons their magic. For what would the story be without
Hánuman's frisking over the roofs of Lanka with his flaming
tail; how much less dramatic the abduction of Sita if she had
not been carried through the sky by her demon captor and
looked down upon the monkeys, Sugriva and Hánuman,
standing on their mountain top!

But it is not the history of this great poem or its captivating story that is its most important aspect. The Ramáyana is a gospel, whose teachings, mostly personified in its principal characters, have been and are now as important as any other of the Hindu scriptures. Rama is an avatar, an incarnation of God, as in a lesser degree are his brothers; Sita is his consort, as woman and as deity. In the Hindu Trinity, God, as the creator, is Brahma; as the protector and maintainer, he is Vishnu; as the destroyer and recreator, he is Shiva. Vishnu is the one who steps in when there is great trouble in heaven or on earth and sets things right. Rama and, later, Krishna are two of his avatars. This idea, of course, entered into and dominated the story long after its inception, as Rama and Sita became more and more loved and admired, as their fame increased, and as the tale, learned by one storyteller from another, told by one generation to the next, was elaborated until it reached its final form.

Rama and Sita are the ideal man and woman, the examples that are held before the vision of Indian boys and girls, men and women. Rama is not a solitary figure, like Buddha and Jesus, who left the ties of home and made their disciples their family; he is the perfect son, brother, husband, warrior, and king, whose example may be followed by those who are concerned with the daily life of the world, as most people are. Sita is the perfect wife and woman, tender, beautiful, and compassionate. Innumerable boys and girls are named after these two; in some places the words of King Jánaka, as he married his daughter to Rama, are a part of the marriage service, and young brides learn by heart the words that Sita spoke to Rama as she followed him in his exile. When Gandhi fell under the assassin's bullet, he cried out, "Ai, Ram!" as a western saint

might say, "O God!" as St. Joan, when the flames reached
her, cried out, "Jesu!"*

This unbroken religious tradition, from the earliest times to
the present day, is strange to us of the West, for our own
tradition was broken irrevocably by the powerful entry of
Christianity into Europe from Asia. The old polytheisms are
gone for good or changed beyond recognition; the epic stories
of the Teutons and the Greeks are, for most of us, relegated to
the bookshelves. But Sita wore a sari, the same beautiful
garment that Indian women wear today. The Indian people
live on the same ground that was trodden by their heroes: they
make pilgrimages to Chitrakuta; to the place whence, it is believed, Sita was carried away by Rávana; and to the great
temple at Rámeswaram, on an island which is part of the
causeway built by the monkeys to Lanka.

The Ramáyana has never ceased to be a vital part of daily
life. It is told by mothers to their children, by storytellers to
rapt, illiterate listeners in towns and villages. In September and
October, in northern India, the festival of Rama is held in
cities and villages and lasts for fifteen days. The Ram Lila, the
play of Rama, is acted out, with great splendor in cities like
Benares and Lahore, crudely and even grotesquely in small
places, but always with devotion and understanding, always
before a delighted audience which knows every speech and
incident and never tires of them. The story traveled wherever
the Indian culture prevailed: into the countries of southeast
Asia and Indonesia. Incidents from it are portrayed in the

---

* In the course of time the final *a* has been dropped from many of
the Sanskrit proper names. The Ramáyana becomes the Ramayan;
Rama, Ram; Bhárata, Bhárat. I have kept the final *a,* fearing that Ram
would be pronounced Răm and that other *a*'s might be shortened.

highly stylized dances of Thailand, Burma, Java, and Bali and in the puppet and shadow plays of Indonesia. They are carved on the walls of Angkor in the exquisite low reliefs of the great Khmer sculptors; there Hánuman may be seen in a wild melee of monkeys and demons.

It seems extraordinary that after centuries of intercourse between East and West a writing of such importance to so many people should be unknown, except to very few, in Europe and America. How many, even among those who are highly educated, know even the names of Rama and Sita? A few years ago, among the Christmas cards issued by UNICEF, there was one with a picture of Sita and the little deer. How many of those who bought the cards in this country knew what was meant by that scene, as familiar to every Hindu as the manger is to us? Yet it is part of our own culture, if we wish to look beyond the Aryan migration into Europe. Besides the pure enjoyment we may gain from the artistry of the story, it behooves us to know the vital elements of the culture of India. For we live, indubitably, in one world, though it is not yet a happy or a brotherly one. Whatever leads to increased understanding between the peoples of that world, to increased delight in each other's unique gifts, should lead to truer unity. This book and its companion were written in the belief that any attempt, however inadequate, to bring these great stories to the attention of Western readers may increase that understanding.

I have taken more liberties with this tale than with the adventures of the Pándavas, for several reasons. The Ramáyana is a much shorter and, in some ways, a thinner narrative than the Mahabhárata, which is so lavish in incident, adventure, and interpolated stories of all kinds that one need only choose between them. In the Ramáyana, for example, ten years of the hero's exile in the forest are recorded with only a statement that the years have passed. To fill out the chapter I have borrowed the lovely story of Savitri from the Mahabhárata, justified, I hope, by the fact that Sita said to Rama that she would follow him as Savitri followed her husband. To explain the purpose of the ascetics' life in the forest I have borrowed, again from the Mahabhárata, an explanation of the search for God.

I am very grateful to the Shanti Sadan, of London, who published the English translation of the Ramáyana by Hari Prasad Shastri, for their permission to use it. Except for a few incidents taken from other versions of the poem, I have used Mr. Shastri's translation.

ELIZABETH SEEGER
Bridgewater, Connecticut
June, 1968

Characters in the Story

Angada: The son of Bali

Bali: King of the Monkeys, son of Indra, God of Heaven

Bhárata: Second son of the King of Koshala

Guha: A ferryman, called the King of the Watermen

Hánuman: A monkey, son of the Wind-God

Indrajita: Son of Rávana

Jámbavan: One of the leaders of the monkeys

Jánaka: King of Mithila

Jatáyu: A vulture

Kaikeyi: Youngest wife of the King of Koshala, mother of Bhárata

Kaushalya: Chief wife of the King of Koshala, mother of Rama

Khara: A brother of Rávana

The King of Koshala

Kumbhakarna: A brother of Rávana

Manthara: Serving maid of Kaikeyi

Maricha: A demon, friend of Rávana

Mátali: The charioteer of Indra

Nala: A monkey who built the causeway to Lanka

Rama: Eldest son of the King of Koshala

Rávana: King of the demons

Sarama: The wife of Vibíshana

Shátrughna and Lákshmana: Twin sons of the King of Koshala

Sita: Daughter of the King of Mithila, wife of Rama

Sugriva: Brother of Bali, son of Surya, the Sun-God

Sumantra: Minister and charioteer of the King of Koshala

Sumitra: Wife of the King of Koshala, mother of Shátrughna and Lákshmana

Surpanakha: Sister of Rávana

Urmila: Sister of Sita, wife of Lákshmana

Vibíshana: A brother of Rávana

Gods in the Story

Agni: God of Fire

Brahma: The Creator, one of the Trinity

Indra: God of Heaven

Vishnu: The Preserver, one of the Trinity

Pronunciation of Proper Names

As a general rule:
>   a = *ah*, as in f*a*ther
>   e = *ay*, as in ob*e*y
>   i = *ee*, as in pol*i*ce
>   o = *o*, as in h*o*le
>   u = *oo*, as in r*u*le
> ai or ay = *y*, as in cr*y*
>   au = *ow*, as in n*ow*

In order to avoid further difficulty, no distinction has been made between the long and short vowels.

Indian names are often accented in a way that Western readers do not expect. It is assumed in this book that proper names are accented on the next-to-last syllable unless otherwise indicated. The exceptions have been given an accent mark on the stressed syllable.

The Ramayana

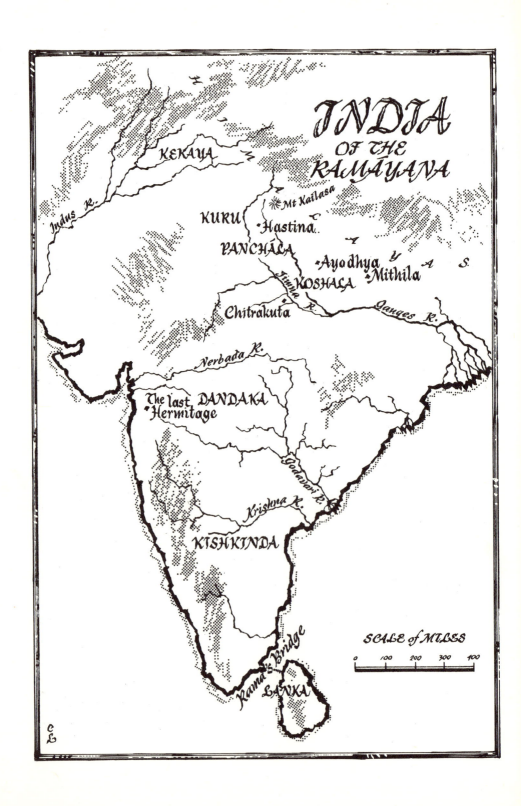

INDIA
OF THE
RAMAYANA

KEKAYA

Indus R.

Mt Kailasa

KURU
•Hastina

PANCHALA
•Ayodhya
KOSHALA •Mithila

Jumna R.
•Chitrakuta
Ganges R.

Nerbada R.

The last DANDAKA
•Hermitage

Godavari R.

Krishna R.

KISHKINDA

SCALE of MILES
0   100   200   300   400

Rama's Bridge
LANKA

1

The Birth of Rama

The gods had met together in the high courts of heaven, for they were troubled. They had a powerful enemy, Rávana, king of the demons, who roamed at will over the three worlds, sometimes fighting and defeating the gods themselves, disturbing the air, the earth and the waters, and scattering the sacrifices of the holy sages who dwelt in the forests. Yet Brahma, the creator of the worlds, the chief of the gods, had granted him the boon that no god or demon or spirit could ever kill him, and therefore no one could put an end to his evil deeds.

It had come about in this way. Rávana had an older brother whom he hated because his brother had been favored by the gods and possessed great wealth and the beautiful kingdom of Lanka, which lay upon an

3

island in the southern ocean. Therefore Rávana began
to control his heart and to conquer his mind and his
body, so that the gods would be pleased and grant him
the power to defeat his brother. He went to the forest
and sat for years in meditation, eating at first the fruit that
fell from the trees within his reach, then eating only the
dry leaves that fell, and finally living on air alone. In
summer he sat between five fires: the sun above him and
four that he kindled on each side of him; in winter and
during the rainy season he sat without shelter, his whole
being concentrated upon this inner discipline. So wise
men do, to purify their hearts and free their souls of sin,
but Rávana's purpose was evil.

Nonetheless, Brahma the creator, seeing him so reso-
lute and so thin, appeared to him and said, "I am pleased
with you, my child. Cease your discipline and ask of me
any boon that you desire, except that you may live forever, for that I may not grant."

And Rávana replied, "Let me never be slain by any god
or demon, spirit or serpent, O lord of creation!"

"You need have no fear of any of those whom you
have named," said Brahma. "Only man shall be able to
kill you."

And Rávana laughed, for he scorned man. Then he
attacked his older brother and drove him from his kingdom, he took over the splendid city of Lanka, which
was built by the divine architect on the summit of a
three-peaked mountain that rose near the island's
shore. From there he ruled over all the demons and
went forth in his arrogance and did much mischief on

earth and in the heavens. His heart was wicked and he rejoiced in his power; he destroyed the pleasure gardens of the gods, carried off nymphs and celestial dancers to Lanka, and his demons raged through the forests, disturbing the sacrifices of the blessed hermits, on whose offerings the gods themselves depended. These demons were the more feared because they devoured men and drank their blood. He descended even into the realm of death and fought against its ruler, Yama; but neither fighter could prevail, since Yama was an immortal and Rávana had been given the boon by Brahma. He went, too, to the bottom of the sea to defy the lord of all the waters and laid waste much of that realm and slew its defenders; but the king was not there and Rávana returned, with shouts of triumph.

At last many of the gods, with the nymphs and spirits of air and water, went to Brahma and besought him, saying, "O god of gods, the demon Rávana is always troubling us and we are helpless before him because of the boon you have granted him. We are terrified by him, for he controls even the sun, the winds, and the seas. Only you can help us."

The lord of the worlds pondered for a while and then said, "I have thought of a plan whereby this evil tyrant may be destroyed. Only man can kill him; therefore he must be destroyed by a man. But that man must have the power of a god."

At this moment the lord Vishnu came among them, the preserver and guardian of the three worlds, equal in power to Brahma, the creator. He rode on his great eagle who is the king of all the birds; he was clad in a gleaming yellow robe, and in three of his four hands he held his conch shell, his mace, and his flaming discus. Brahma told him of the gods' distress and their only hope of deliverance. The lesser deities worshiped him with the palms of their hands joined together, and they implored him, "O guardian of all creatures, we beg you to be born of man in order to destroy Rávana, the scourge of earth and heaven."

"Fear no more!" answered Vishnu. "Be at peace, for I shall slay Rávana with his friends and kinsmen and all his army. But where shall I take birth as man?"

All who heard him rejoiced, and the God of Fire, Agni, said to him, "The good and wise king of Koshala is even now preparing a sacrifice in order to obtain a son. Be born, O conqueror of foes, as sons to his three wives and free us from our fears."

The lord Vishnu graciously agreed, and then Brahma spoke again to the assembled gods and to the nymphs and spirits of the forest and the waters and the air to whom Rávana had done great harm. "Since the blessed Vishnu is willing to be born of man for your sakes, you must help him by begetting great sons among the monkeys of the southern forest. Anyone who attacks Rávana in his stronghold of Lanka must pass that way and will need the help of those who know the forest best. Be born as monkeys, skilled in magic, swift as the wind, able to change their shape at will as demons do, to cleave rocks and mountains and to fly in the air like eagles."

Thus the prayers of the gods were answered.

Agni, the lord of fire, had spoken truly, for in the beautiful city of Ayodhya the king of Koshala was preparing a great sacrifice.

Now Koshala was a prosperous and happy kingdom in the northern part of that great country that is called India today. Its capital city was built on the bank of a river that flows into the sacred Ganges; it was called Ayodhya, which means "not to be fought against." Its walls were strong and its moat deep; its gates were arched like thunderclouds, and it was protected by warriors who never fled from a foe. Within the walls were spacious houses and lovely gardens, pools of clear water, and blossoming trees, wide streets that were daily sprinkled with water and strewn with flowers. There were ample stables for the war elephants and for those on which the king and his friends often rode; also for the many horses that the warriors rode or yoked to their chariots, and houses for those chariots and for all the gear of war.

Many learned men and priests lived there who studied the holy books, the Vedas, and who were able to perform the rites and sacrifices. Poets and musicians, actors and dancers, made the city beautiful and gay. The markets and shops were filled with every sort of ware made by skilled craftsmen: weavers and goldsmiths, jewelers and potters, carpenters and carvers; workers in glass and ivory, perfumers, incense makers, and those who made fans of peacock feathers. The farmers outside the walls raised plenty of grain and the cattle were round and sleek; for the rains were abundant and dams were built

in the right places to hold the precious water during the
dry season.

The king cherished all the four castes: the Brahmans
who were the priests and counselors and teachers; the
Kshatrias who were the rulers and the warriors; the
Vaisyas who were merchants, traders, and farmers; and
the Shudras who were the servants of all. Each man
worked happily at his own trade and prospered. There
was no poverty or thievery; every family had a pleasant
house and garden; every man and woman wore earrings
and a necklace; none went hungry and no son died before his father.

The kingdom was a happy one because its ruler was
wise. Men follow the example of their king; if they are
dealt with justly, they in turn are just. In his handsome
palace, the king of Koshala ruled as Indra does in heaven.
He had studied the Vedas; he loved the truth and never
broke his word; he was a great warrior, but was a friend
to all and loved by his people. His high priest and
teacher was a great sage, one of the wisest in the world,
and he chose able and honest ministers. Three loving and
lovely queens dwelt in the inner realm of his palace. He
had only one sorrow: he had no son to succeed him and
to carry on the line of his ancestors.

Therefore at this time he said to his high priest, "I
pray you, O holy one, to prepare the sacrifice that will
bring me a son, and to perform it according to the sacred
traditions set forth in the Vedas."

"So be it!" answered the priest; and he summoned
Brahmans and architects, workmen, musicians, and

dancers. "Measure off a level piece of land on the north bank of the river and raise the sacrificial pavilion," he said to the builders. "Then build all around it handsome dwellings for those kings and Brahmans and warriors who will be invited to the ceremony. Fill these houses with every comfort and with food for men and horses and elephants. Let all be done with good will and courtesy, and let no one suffer during this holy time so that the purpose of the king's sacrifice may be accomplished."

Messengers were sent to all the neighboring kings, who came with their priests and their warriors and were made welcome. The whole city was dressed with flags and garlands of flowers, and every citizen wore his finest robe and ornaments. The streets were sprinkled with perfume, and the sound of drums and music never ceased. Gifts of food and apparel, jewels and gold were given freely to all the castes.

When all was ready the sacrifice was held; the sacred fire was lighted and each day the offerings and libations were presented without a fault by Brahmans well versed in the Vedas, directed by the high priest.

On the last day there was a sound like the throbbing of a great drum, and out of the sacred fire appeared a majestic figure clad in a red robe and flashing jewels. He held in his hand a golden vessel with a silver cover, and he spoke to the king in a voice as deep as thunder: "Receive the fruit of your sacrifice, O King! The celestial food in this dish has been prepared by the gods and will give you your heart's desire. Let your queens partake of it and they will bear your sons."

The king took the golden vessel and raised it to his
forehead, worshiping the god, who forthwith vanished
from his sight. Then, rejoicing as a penniless man who
has just received a fortune, he entered the inner apartments of his palace. He went to the first and most honored of his queens and gave her half of the heavenly
food; then he divided the rest of it in two equal parts
and gave one to each of the other queens, and all of them
consumed it with great joy.

In the spring when all the favorable planets were
alight, the queens brought forth their sons. The firstborn
was the child of that mother who had eaten half of the
celestial food, and great was the rejoicing at his birth. A
few days later a second son was born, and then the third
queen gave birth to twin boys, and the king's joy was
complete. The city and indeed the whole kingdom, as
the news spread, was one great festival. Poets and min-
strels sang the praise of father and sons; dancers and
acrobats entertained the people, and the streets resounded
with music and laughter. The eldest boy was named
Rama, the "delight" of his parents and the world; the
second was Bhárata, the "upholder" of the kingdom;
and the twins were Lákshmana, the "fortunate," and
Shátrughna, "conqueror of foes."

The boys were all strong and handsome. Rama and
Bhárata were dark-skinned as storm clouds, the twins
fairer; all had black, curling hair and eyes as large as
lotus leaves, dark and bright. They learned all the
branches of knowledge under the wisest of their father's
counselors; the most skillful of his warriors taught them

the use of every weapon, for they belonged to the Kshatria caste who are the protectors and rulers of men and must ever be ready for war. They became excellent riders and were skillful in driving the chariot; they learned to use the bow, the sword, and the mace. They practiced, as they grew older, in the hunt and in games together and with their friends, and the citizens loved to watch the young princes as they raced with gay voices and laughter on the land outside the walls or competed in archery, each arrow marked with its owner's name.

The brothers were devoted to one another and were almost always together; but if they separated or took sides in a game, Lákshmana always went with Rama and Shátrughna with Bhárata. As they rode through the city or went hither and yon at their father's behest, they were seen thus in pairs; in each pair, one was dark and one fair. Among them Rama was always the leader, because he was the eldest and also because he was the strongest and the wisest; for he possessed half of the nature of Vishnu, while the others had a lesser portion. He was skilled in all the arts of peace and war, especially in archery, for no one could surpass him in the use of the bow.

One day, when the boys were about fifteen years old, the king was seated in his court among his counselors when the porter of the city gate was admitted to his presence. A great sage, he said, stood at the gate; he had given his name to the porter and desired to see the king. When the king heard the name he rose at once and with his high priest went on foot to welcome the illustrious visitor who was, indeed, one of the holiest of wise men. The king knelt before him and took the dust from his feet, for a man who left the world and went into the woods to purify his heart and seek the truth was honored far more than those who dwelt in palaces. Then the sage was taken to the palace where his feet were washed and milk and rice and honey offered to him for refreshment.

After the usual courteous questions were asked and answered, the king said, "O sinless one, your coming is a joy and blessing to me, like rain falling on parched earth. Be pleased to tell me why you have come and what is your will. I will do anything you ask of me."

"I have come a long way from my forest hermitage, great King, to ask a favor of you," answered his guest. "When I perform a sacrifice in that place, after assembling all the necessary offerings, after fulfilling every rite for several days, just when the sacrifice has reached its height, a great demon, with a host of followers, comes rushing down and scatters the offerings and defiles the altar. They are sent by Rávana, the king of all demons, who dwells in Lanka and sends his minions forth to trouble us. I may not destroy or even curse them, because at the time of sacrifice no violence may be done and no anger felt.

"Therefore, O King, lend me your son Rama to destroy those demons. Only he can do it, and because of their sins they will not be able to stand against him. Do not let a father's love prevent you; give me your dear son for the space of ten days, so that I may complete my sacrifice."

The king's heart was stricken by these words, and he lay back, trembling, upon his throne. When he could speak, he answered the sage, "O holy one, my Rama is but fifteen years old and has no experience of war. How can he slay demons who are so powerful and wicked? The gods themselves cannot destroy Rávana; how can I send my son to contend with his followers? I have a great army and seasoned warriors whom I myself will lead against your foes, but I will not let this young child go; O blessed one, I cannot give my son!"

The sage was enraged by these words: he rose and his flashing eyes were terrible to behold, for the anger of a saint is hard to bear. "Remember, O King, that you were born of a noble house!" he said. "How can you dare to break your word? You said that you would do anything that I asked of you. If this is your decision, I shall take my leave and you may stay here with your sons and your army, O breaker of promises!"

The palace trembled under his wrath, but the high priest of the king, that holy one who was his spiritual teacher, spoke soothing words to the monarch: "After following the path of virtue all your life, do not abandon it now and break your word, O lord of men. He who breaks his word destroys his honor. You need not fear to send your son; no harm can come to him in the presence of this wise one who before he retired to the forest was a mighty king. He has no equal in knowledge and discipline; all things in the past, present, and future are known to him. He has mastered all weapons, human and divine, and could slay the demons in the wink of an eye if he had not taken up the holy life. It will be for Rama's own good to go with him."

The king accepted this wise counsel and sent for Rama, who came with Lákshmana following him. Their father embraced them both and gave them into the care of the sage. Then they girded on their swords, slung their quivers on their shoulders, and taking their bows in their hands, followed the sage out of the city, along the bank of the river.

The King Receives the Golden Vessel

2

The First Adventures

The sage led the way along the river southward, Rama walking behind him and Lákshmana following. When evening came, he told them where berries and succulent roots could be found for their food, and they gathered fruits for the holy one and themselves. They bathed in the river and said their evening prayers. Then, since the brothers were not used to sleeping on the ground, they gathered armfuls of grass and made beds, where they all slept soundly.

On the second day they came to a dark, entangled forest where the roars of beasts and the harsh cries of flesh-eating birds could be heard. There were no paths through it and no man seemed to dwell there. "Why is this forest so dark and terrifying, O wise one?" asked

Rama. "Only beasts seem to live here, and it is a wilderness of trees and creepers."

"It was once a pleasant land, my son, with prosperous cities and cultivated fields," said the sage, "but a perverse demon came here and devastated it because it was the abode of a holy hermit who had once cursed him. He plundered the cities and blocked the roads, and the people all left for fear of him. You can slay him, O Rama, and free this land; he lives not far from here. Come, let us enter the forest and find him."

"I will do whatever you command me to do," answered Rama. "For that purpose I have come here."

He and Lákshmana strung their bows and Rama plucked his bowstring with a twang that made the beasts flee to their dens and the birds scatter like leaves in the wind. The demon heard it and came roaring out in a fury, but the brothers met him with a shower of arrows that sent him back into hiding. From behind the trees he threw out clouds of dust and a shower of stones. Rama drew from his quiver arrows that could follow sound, and these, flowing like serpents through the air, found the demon and wounded him. He rushed forth again, and with one powerful arrow Rama pierced his heart.

They spent the night in the forest, which now was filled with peace and the songs of birds. The sage had seen the fearlessness and prowess of the two lads, and in the morning he said to them, "I am pleased with you, my children. Now I will show you the use of divine weapons, given me by the gods in former times. With these you can conquer all your enemies, whether gods, demons, or serpents. Listen to me carefully!" They bathed and purified themselves and sat beside their master with all their being concentrated on what he told them.

"With these spells you can summon weapons that can destroy or turn aside any missile sent against you and slay him who sent it," he said. "This one," and he taught it to them, "will bring you the Wind-God's power, and this the blast of Agni, the Fire-God, that none can stand against. This one will bring to your hand the thunderbolt of Indra and this a shaft that will put your enemies to sleep. This weapon is invisible, this one will take any form that you desire; and here is the very noose of death."

As he spoke the spells the weapons appeared and stood obediently beside him. Some shone like fire, others were dark as smoke. He showed the two brothers how to use them and made them repeat again and again the words that would summon and dismiss them. "Do not use them against any human foe," the master said. "But against demons who are skilled in magic and have more than human power, use them freely."

The spirits of the weapons bowed to Rama and said, "We are at your service, O prince. What would you have us do?"

"When I need you I will summon you," answered Rama. "Come to me then and serve me well."

Then the weapons vanished, and the boys followed the sage, amazed and grateful, for they need not now fear any demon.

The next day they arrived at their teacher's hermitage, a lovely clearing in the forest where the birds were singing and the deer browsed unafraid. The huts of many hermits stood among the trees, and the holy men came out to welcome the travelers and offer them food, and water to wash their feet.

When they had rested, Rama asked the sage, "Who are these holy ones whose faces shine with an inner light, who live in this lovely hermitage with you, O sinless one? I know that you ruled a splendid kingdom. Who were these and why did they come here?"

"Many of them were Brahmans, like the priests and learned men in your father's court, O Rama," answered the sage, "and some were Kshatrias, warriors or kings, for it is fitting for a man, when his hair is white and his sons are grown, to leave the world and enter the forest. Here he frees himself from sin, through fasting and discipline, and gives his heart and mind to the search for God, that God who is above all gods, who can never be perceived by any sense, the Invisible, the Unmanifest, the knowledge of whom is bliss."

"How can a man gain that knowledge, O fountain of wisdom?" asked Rama.

"He must give up all the desires that dwell in the heart, and rid himself also of fear and anger, O virtuous prince," answered the sage. "The knowledge of God is found in the cave of the heart, which must be pure of any other purpose. A man must withdraw his mind from all the things that his senses perceive, as a tortoise withdraws his limbs and head into his shell. Heat and cold, pain and pleasure, praise and blame, joy and sorrow are the same to him. Controlled, disciplined, silent, he must find his joy within himself, not in outward things. Only thus can he find God; in his own self he finds that highest Self.

"Then he knows that Self to be present in all other beings as it is in him; he sees himself in all creatures and all creatures in himself. He has no fear and no desire and enters into peace and bliss. It is this union with God that the forest dwellers seek; it is this, when they obtain it, that makes their faces shine with inner radiance."

That evening after the sage had retired to meditate, his disciples told the two princes about their master. "He was a powerful king," said one of them, "for he was learned in all the branches of knowledge, he cared about the welfare of his people and was an unconquerable warrior.

"One time he assembled his army and went forth to tour his own domain and to visit other kings. He also paid obeisance to the holy ones who dwell in the forests, and he came one day to the hermitage of that saint who is now your father's teacher and high priest, O noble princes. The saint received him graciously and they talked together for a long time. When the king rose to take his leave, the blessed one said, 'You have a large retinue and an army with you, who have waited patiently while we talked. I wish to offer them hospitality and beg you to accept the little that I have to give.' The king demurred, but finally had to yield to the saint's insistence.

"Then the holy one called for his favorite spotted cow,

Shabala, and said to her, 'Draw near and listen, O dear one! I wish to offer hospitality to the king and all his army and retainers. You are the wish-fulfilling cow; therefore bring forth splendid dishes which will be pleasing to them.'

"The cow provided all that could be desired: heaps of hot rice, milk, honey, wine, and sweets of all kinds, and the king and his priests, his ministers and his warriors partook of it all with great pleasure. After they had feasted, the king said, 'I beg of you to give me this cow, Shabala, O fortunate one, and I will give you in exchange a thousand excellent cows. Shabala is a jewel and jewels belong to kings and not to forest dwellers.'

" 'I would not part with Shabala for a million other cows, nor for mountains of gold and silver,' answered the saint. 'She provides for all who live here and enables me to entertain the gods themselves. She furnishes alms for all who come and offerings for my sacrifices; she is my very life and fulfills all my needs. I cannot give her up.' The king offered a thousand elephants adorned with golden trappings, a hundred chariots each drawn by four white horses, innumerable cows of varied colors, and much gold. But the holy one refused to give up his beloved Shabala.

"When the king left, he ordered his soldiers to carry her off by force. But Shabala, bellowing with grief, shook off her captors and ran back and knelt before her master, tears falling from her eyes. 'How have I offended you, my lord, and why have you cast me off? Why are the king's soldiers dragging me from the hermitage?' she asked. 'I have not cast you off, my dear one,' said her master, speaking to her as if she were his sister. 'The king is drunk with desire for you, and how can I defend you? He is a warrior with a mighty army, stronger than I am.'

"Now Shabala had often listened to the reading of the Vedas and she was skilled in argument. 'The power of a warrior is as nothing compared to that of a saint,' she answered. 'Allow me, my lord, to destroy the pride of this wicked wretch.' Her master gave her leave, and she produced a great army that put the royal army to flight. The king was shamed by this defeat; he was like a bird without wings, a snake bereft of its fangs, the sun in eclipse. He gave his kingdom to his eldest son and went into the forest in order to acquire the power that the holy man possessed.

"For many years he disciplined his mind and body, eating less and less until he lived on air alone, standing in summer between five fires, without shelter during the rains, and in water during the winter. The gods beheld his efforts, and the great god Shiva, the giver of boons, went to him and asked him what he desired. 'O adorable one, teach me the use of the divine weapons used by the gods,' answered the former king. The god granted the boon and so it was that he posssessed those celestial missiles that he put into your hands, O Rama, for he has no use for them now.

"Our master had not yet conquered his passions," continued the disciple. "He desired the weapons so that he might overcome the saint who had refused to give him Shabala. So he went to the hermitage and flung the Fire-

God's weapon into the forest, setting it ablaze. Many of the hermits and disciples, as well as the birds and beasts, fled before the flames, but the saint stood firm and came to meet his enemy with only his staff in his hand. 'How can your power compare with that of the spirit, O vilest of warriors?' he cried. 'O stupid one, loose all your weapons against this staff of mine!' The angry king flung all the weapons that Shiva had given him, but they were all destroyed by the staff of the holy one, from whose body light poured forth and whose staff shone like fire. The king was again defeated, and this time he realized what had overcome him. He repented of his greed and his enmity; he gave up his anger and purified his heart, after many years of spiritual labor.

"Then the gods raised him from the Kshatria caste to the Brahman; he was reconciled to his former enemy and became our revered master, teaching and performing sacrifices and doing much good."

Rama and Lákshmana were delighted with this story and slept happily in the hermitage that night.

The next morning Rama said, "Begin your sacrifice when you will, O blessed one, and we shall protect it against the demons. May good fortune attend it!"

The ceremony was begun that very day. "Keep watch over this place for six days, my sons," their teacher said. "After that the rite will be completed and the danger past."

The two brothers watched for five days with their bows in their hands, their swords at their sides, and in their minds the divine weapons that they could call upon.

They slept in turn, and were fed by the hermits with the fruit and roots of the forest; they never lost sight of the altar and its sacred flame. On the sixth day Rama said to Lákshmana, "We must be ready today. Let us summon the divine weapons, for we shall need them." They repeated the spells and the weapons appeared at their sides, none too soon; for even as Rama spoke the altar fire flared and wavered; a clamor arose from the woods and a powerful demon roared like a tornado out of the sky, followed by a host of others. The leader was named Maricha and was one of the most trusted friends and ministers of Rávana himself.

Rama struck the breast of Maricha with the thunderbolt of Indra, flinging his body far over the forest. Lákshmana pierced another's heart with fire, and then, with the Wind-God's weapon, they scattered the rest a hundred miles away. The battle was soon over and the two boys smiled at one another, delighted with the power of their new weapons. The sacrifice was completed; peace was brought to the hermitage, and all those who dwelt there blessed and praised the young heroes.

After resting in that pleasant place, fragrant with blossoms and sweet with the songs of birds, Rama said to the sage, "We are your servants, O master. Have you further need of us? We are here to obey you."

"The city of the just King Jánaka is not far from here," answered the sage. "He is performing a sacrifice which many of us wish to attend. Go with us, O princes! The king owns a rare and wonderful bow, given him by the gods. It is very heavy and splendid and no man can

even lift it, much less string it, though many have tried.
Go with us to the sacrifice and you shall behold this
bow."

Many of the hermits and their disciples went with the
master; the birds, the deer, and the monkeys also followed him, until he asked them to return to the hermitage. The two brothers rejoiced in the journey, for they
had never before been outside their own kingdom. They
crossed rivers, sometimes by a ford, sometimes by a ferry;
they rested in hermitages, walked through fertile lands,
passed through the busy streets of towns and spent one
night as the king's guests in his beautiful and prosperous
city.

When they reached the city of Jánaka they were welcomed with joy by the king, who begged the sage to take
the place of honor in his court. Rama and Lákshmana
stood apart, side by side, dressed in yellow robes with
golden necklaces and bracelets, and armed with their
swords and bows. "Who are these two young princes,
beautiful as gods, majestic as elephants, who came with
you, O wisest of men?" asked the king. "Tell me, whose
sons are they?"

The sage told him who they were and how they had
slain the demons and saved his hermitage, and the king
welcomed them with honor. Then the sage said, "These
young warriors wish to see the great bow that the gods
have given you, O King, if you will permit them to do
so."

"I will show it to them gladly," answered the king,
"and if either one of them can lift and string it, I will

give my daughter Sita to him in marriage. This daughter is very precious to me. She is very beautiful and has a tender heart and a sweet nature; she was not born of mortal man and woman. Some years ago I was preparing for the rites of spring, and I myself plowed the land for the ceremony. As I opened one furrow, there in the dust lay a baby girl. I took her in my arms and brought her home, and my wife received her with joy, for she was a lovely child. She has grown up as my daughter and I have named her Sita, the furrow, after her birthplace; for she seemed like the very daughter of the earth, a goddess of the spring.

"When she was old enough to marry I resolved that no ordinary man should wed her, but only one who could bend the mighty bow. So I announced that my daughter was ready for marriage and that any man of noble birth might compete for her hand. Many kings and princes assembled here and we held high festival, but not one of them could even lift the bow. And when they saw the beauty of the maiden, as she came forth holding the bridal garland, and none could win it, they were filled with rage. After they left my kingdom they banded together and came back and besieged my city for a year, resolved to carry her off by force. But I fought them off, at great cost to my city and my treasury. Now let these princes try their strength!"

He ordered the bow to be brought. Many men together lifted the iron chest in which it lay, put it on a cart and pulled it with difficulty into a courtyard of the palace. The news of this new trial flew through the city,

and many people ran to the palace and crowded round
to see what might happen. Rama stepped forward,
opened the iron chest and looked at the bow. He grasped
it at the center, lifted it easily, and picked up the bowstring. Resting one end of the mighty bow against his
foot and putting forth all his strength, he bent it toward
him to string it, and lo, under his hands, it cracked in
two with a sound like a thunderbolt that echoed through
the city. Those far away heard it and cried, "The bow is
strung!" And those nearby cried out, "The bow is
broken!"

King Jánaka, amazed and delighted, embraced Rama
and said to him, "I will give to you the hand of my
daughter Sita, who is dearer to me than my life. Now
let us send with all haste messengers to your father, asking him to come hither to give his consent to this marriage and to be present at your wedding." Then he
turned to the younger brother, saying, "O Lákshmana, I
have a younger daughter who is also fair and virtuous.
Do you take her hand in marriage, if you so desire."

In Ayodhya nothing had been heard from the two
princes since they had set out on their dangerous journey
with the sage. Now messengers on swift horses, tired by
three days of speedy travel, arrived at the gate and were
admitted to the king's presence. "O illustrious King,"
they said, "the ruler of Mithila, King Jánaka, sends his
affectionate greetings and these good tidings: your two
noble sons are at his court, well and happy. His daughter
Sita has been won by your eldest son, Rama, who broke

the sacred bow which no other man has even been able
to lift. The king begs that you will consent to this marriage and also to that of his younger daughter, Urmila, to
Prince Lákshmana. Come with all speed to his city, O
ruler of men, with your counselors, your kinsmen, and
your attendants, to witness the wedding of your children!"

The king was overjoyed at this good news, as were his
queens and his sons Bhárata and Shátrughna. "Let us
set out tomorrow," said he. "Load many carts with gold
and jewels, with fine apparel, and golden and silver
vessels! Make ready the royal chariot and litters to bring
home the brides and their attendants; bring horses and
elephants for my counselors and ministers, and let a
division of the army go with us!"

This fine company, with banners flying from its
chariots, with elephants and horses richly caparisoned,
spent four nights on the journey and arrived on the fifth
morning at the city of Jánaka, which was gaily dressed
for the coming festival. It was fragrant with flowers and
incense and resounded with music; the citizens in their
best attire lined the streets, and the ladies leaned from
their windows and terraces to greet the guests. The king
welcomed them warmly, giving his royal visitor rich
apartments for himself and his counselors and housing
the army and its animals in comfort. Father and sons
met with joy, and the four brothers were happy to be
together again.

Now the brother of Jánaka, king of a neighboring
realm, had come for the weddings, and when he saw

Rama and Lákshmana he wished that he had two such
bridegrooms for his own fair daughters. Then Bhárata
and Shátrughna appeared, as handsome and strong as
their brothers, and he desired them as sons-in-law, thinking himself fortunate that four such youths existed in the
world. He consulted the two kings and the princes; the
marriages were arranged and the maidens sent for. The
brothers were delighted that all of them would be
wedded at the same time.

The wedding festivities began, with bards and min-
strels praising both noble families. There were plays and
dances in the courtyards and in the streets, acrobats and
musicians entertained the citizens, and countless lamps
and torches made the nights as merry as the days. The
king of Koshala and all of his company were feasted, and
both they and King Jánaka gave away rich gifts of jewels
and precious apparel.

On the third day the sacred fire was lighted and the
priests of both royal houses dressed the altar with flowers
and lighted the pots of incense. King Jánaka's kinsmen
and courtiers, his counselors and ministers, as well as all
those who had come from Koshala, crowded the hall,
waiting for the four young couples to appear. Rama and
his brothers entered in rich attire, with wedding crowns,
flashing earrings, and jeweled armlets, looking like
young gods, and Rama was foremost among them. From
the other side the four maidens appeared, in robes of
flower-colored silk, their golden girdles and anklets set
with little bells that sounded gently as they moved, their
shining hair crowned with jeweled headdresses. Al-

though they looked as lovely as celestial nymphs, they walked with modest steps and downcast eyes, for they were shy in the presence of so many people. Among them the great beauty of Sita shone as the moon does among the stars.

Then Rama took a seat by the sacred fire and Sita sat opposite him. She raised her eyes and they looked at one another across the flame and each gave to the other a heart full of love. "O Rama," said King Jánaka, "from this day my daughter Sita will be your companion on the path of virtue. Faithful and tender, she will follow you as if she were your shadow. Accept her, and take her hand in yours. May you both be happy!"

Then Jánaka called Lákshmana and married him to Sita's younger sister, and Bhárata and Shátrughna wed the two fair cousins. "Be gentle and faithful to your wives, as they will be to you, O princes of Koshala," said King Jánaka. "Receive them now and take their hands." The four brothers each took the hand of his bride; they walked three times around the fire, and the ceremony was completed by the priests according to the holy rules set down in the Vedas.

When all was done, the wedding guests, weary with happiness, left the city. That great sage who had given Rama the celestial weapons and who had brought about these happy weddings, blessed them all and took his leave, for he was going to the Himalayas to meditate in their vast solitudes. The king of Koshala also prepared to leave with his sons and their brides. The carts full of treasure that he had brought with him had been emptied by generous hands, and their contents given to Jánaka and his queens, to his priests and courtiers, and to the citizens. Now they were filled high again by Jánaka with dowry for his daughters. In addition to the gold and jewels and fine raiment, he gave mighty elephants with painted heads and trunks and fine seats fastened to their broad backs; swift horses and handsome chariots; maidservants for the princesses and men for their husbands. A great procession of people and animals went back to Ayodhya, where they were eagerly awaited.

Great was the delight of the people as they saw the four princes riding their prancing horses and the litters that carried their brides; and great was the joy of the three queens as they saw their sons again and took into their arms the lovely girls whom they welcomed as dear daughters. Again, as at the birth of those four brothers, high festival was held in that happy city that seemed to know no sorrow.

3
Manthara's Evil Design

For twelve years after their marriages, Rama and his brothers lived happily in Ayodhya. They helped their father in the government of his kingdom, for he was an old man when they were born. Rama, especially, kept watch over all the people and saw to it that their needs were satisfied. He cared for them as if they were his children, helping the unfortunate, comforting those who were in distress, rejoicing with them in their festivals. Occasionally there was warfare on the borders or a raid by lawless men who envied the wealth of Koshala. Then Rama led his father's army to battle, with his three brothers beside him, and no enemy could stand against them. They obeyed the sage and used no divine weapon against men, but their skill in archery, their use of the

sword and the mace, the maneuvering of their chariots
and their mastery of riding either horses or elephants
made them unconquerable warriors. All the people felt
safe with these young princes to protect them; they knew
that when the old king died, Rama would succeed him,
and they loved and trusted him beyond all men.

At home the brothers were obedient to their father and
looked upon all three queens as their mothers, making
no difference between them. They were happy in their
marriages. Sita, beautiful and gentle, was the joy of
Rama's life and he of hers. She knew her husband's
thoughts before he told them to her and did everything
to please him, and her love for him filled every moment
of her life.

In the thirteenth year the king, seeing Rama as
resplendent as the full moon and beloved of the people,
decided to make him regent as well as heir to the kingdom. He was weary of the burden of government; he
wished to lay it on the strong shoulders of his son and to
see Rama crowned before he himself should die.

He called together his ministers and the elders of the
people; he summoned also the rulers of those kingdoms
that were subject to him, and when all were arrived,
they assembled in his court, facing the royal throne where
the king sat, looking like Indra among the gods.

"I have ruled this empire for many years and am now
grown old and weary," he told them. "I have performed
hundreds of sacrifices and have done my duty to the
gods, to my ancestors and to men. Now, with your consent, I wish to give the protection of this dominion to

my eldest son, Rama. If this seems right to you, give me your consent or say what shall otherwise be done."

They cried out in joyful agreement; but the king, wishing to make still more sure of their intent, asked them again, "You have accepted my suggestion gladly; but tell me truly why you wish to see Rama crowned."

Those who were present consulted together and chose a spokesman who said, "You are fortunate to have such a son, O mighty one. You have been the greatest ruler of your line, but none is so virtuous as Rama. His fame is already widespread and his splendor increases every day. In warfare he is more powerful than the gods; he never returns from battle until his enemy is defeated. Yet he never glories in his power or uses it unjustly. He loves the truth and will never break his word, whatever happens. He is as forgiving as the earth; he never speaks ill of others and is free from pride and jealousy; he is self-controlled, courteous, humble and wise. Yet he knows how to punish the evildoer even as he shows mercy to the innocent. He honors the wise and the aged. He is learned in the Vedas and in all knowledge and is skilled in the arts of music and painting. That mighty archer, lover of the truth, the servant of the people, blesses all who seek his protection and is always righteous.

"The people of the whole kingdom, at dawn and eventide, pray for his life and happiness. Truly, as his name declares, he has become the delight of the world. O giver of boons, we beg you to crown Rama without delay. We long to see him riding upon the royal elephant, under the white canopy."

These words filled the king's heart with joy. He sent for Rama, who entered that assembly, bowed low before his father and touched his feet. The king seated his son beside him on the throne and told him what had been decided. "So be it, my father!" answered Rama. "May all your desires be fulfilled!"

The kings and ministers acclaimed him, and then his father dismissed them all, keeping only his chief priest beside him. "It is for you, O blessed one, to arrange all that is necessary for the coming ceremony," he said.

The priest told the king's ministers to bring gold and silver, jewels, garlands of white flowers, white flags, a white canopy, and fly-whisks made of yaks' tails; rice, butter and honey in separate vessels of gold shining like fire; a chariot spread with a tigerskin; elephants free of any imperfection, and bulls with gilded horns. All these were to be brought to the king's sacrificial pavilion where the coronation would take place. Food and gifts must also be prepared for all the Brahmans in the city and for those who had come with the visiting kings. He then gave orders for the decoration of the city.

Meanwhile the news, like a flock of birds, had flown through all the palace windows and over the city, and when Rama returned home the streets were full of happy people who greeted him with joy as he passed by and who, when they returned to their homes, prayed to their household gods that nothing might stand in the way of his coronation.

No sooner had he entered his palace than, to his surprise, he was again summoned by his father.

He found the king uneasy and troubled. "O my son," his father said, "it is my desire and that of all the people that you become regent and rule this land. I have had fearful dreams; the star of my birth is in a dangerous position and evil omens have been seen by my priests, who say that they foretell the death of a king or some great misfortune. O blessed one, I wish to see you crowned before I die. Tomorrow, the astrologers say, a favorable star will arise; therefore I wish to have you proclaimed regent in the morning at dawn."

"But my brothers Bhárata and Shátrughna are not here, my father," answered Rama. "It is many months since they went to visit Bhárata's grandsire. Should we not wait for them?"

"It is my desire that it be done tomorrow," said the old king. "Tonight you and Sita must fast, lying on a bed of grass, with a stone for a pillow. Go now, my son, and prepare yourself."

When Rama returned home he did not find Sita there, so he went on to his mother's palace. There Sita and Lákshmana were sitting with his mother in her temple, meditating with closed eyes and controlled breathing, and praying for him, for they had heard of the king's decree. They welcomed him with joy, talking happily together of the coming event. "Share with me the government of our kingdom," Rama said to his brother. "It is as much yours as mine, for you are my second self." Then he told them that he and Sita must fast that night and she returned with him to their own palace. A bed of sacred grass was laid down for them in their temple, and after they had purified themselves they observed the vow of fasting and silence and, when night came, they lay down to sleep.

Meanwhile the city was in a turmoil of joy and excitement. Men were erecting arches over the principal streets and women were making garlands of flowers to decorate them. It was spring and the trees and flowers were in full bloom. Every house was gay with banners and flowers, and everyone was shouting and laughing; even the children were helping and talking about Rama. The royal kitchens were busy all day and night, for many people were to be feasted and cooling drinks and cakes were to be served at the crossroads. Soldiers polished their arms and armor, groomed the horses and painted with auspicious designs the head and trunk of the royal elephant on which Rama would ride, under the white canopy of kingship, while jeweled fans and snowwhite yak tails were waved about him. As the news spread, the roads into Ayodhya were crowded with people, and the streets were so full that it was hard to pass through them.

Now Bhárata's mother, Queen Kaikeyi, had a serving-maid who had been with her all her life; her name was Manthara; she was humpbacked and of an evil disposition, though devoted to her mistress. In the late afternoon she heard all the noise arising from the streets and stepped out on a balcony to see what it was all about. Beholding the festivity, she looked for someone who could tell her the cause and met a servant of Rama's mother gaily dressed in silken garments.

"Is it the mother of Rama who is giving away lavish gifts?" asked Manthara. "Why are the people so happy?"

"Tomorrow at dawn the king will crown Prince Rama as regent," was the answer.

Manthara was filled with jealousy and rage. She hurried to the room where her mistress was resting.

"Why are you lying there, O foolish one?" she cried. "Do you not know that a dire misfortune has befallen you, that you are in great danger?"

"What misfortune, what danger, O Manthara?" asked the queen. "Why do you look so wild?"

"Listen to me!" answered Manthara. "The king has announced that Prince Rama will be crowned regent at dawn tomorrow. I am filled with dread, O my Queen; I am as if scorched by fire, for your woes are my woes, your danger my danger. This deceitful king, who has always told you how much he loved you, has now exalted the mother of Rama and will destroy you and your son."

"You have brought me joyful news, O kind one," said the beautiful queen, smiling. "I am delighted to hear of Rama's coronation, for he is as dear to me as Bhárata and I make no difference between them. Take this as thanks." And she unclasped a jewel from her arm and gave it to the hunchback.

But Manthara threw it angrily on the ground. "O stupid queen," she cried. "This is no time for rejoicing. Bhárata has as good a right to the throne as his brother; Rama fears him and therefore, while he is away at your father's court, seizes the crown. The king's mother is honored above all other queens; after this you will wait upon Rama's mother like a servant, and your son, too, will be no better than a slave to his elder brother. Knowing all this, I tremble for you!"

"Rama is the eldest son, O hunchback," said the queen. "He is the one to be regent and heir to his father. Why are you so jealous of him? He will always honor and protect his brothers, for he loves them as he does himself. When he is crowned, there will be four kings."

"You are sinking in an ocean of misery and still you cannot see it," said her servant. "When Rama becomes king, your son will be like an orphan and you will be a slave. Rama loves Lákshmana as he does himself, but he fears Bhárata and will surely either banish him or put him to death. It would be best for him to escape now to the forest. Remember, O beautiful one, that you have often slighted Rama's mother because you were the king's favorite. Do you think she will spare you, when she is the mother of the king?

"O mistress, there is still time. I know a way by which Bhárata may be crowned and Rama banished to the forest."

Manthara's evil words had penetrated the queen's heart as a poisonous serpent glides into a bedchamber. She frowned and bit her nether lip. "How could Bhárata become king and Rama be banished?" she asked at last.

"Do you remember that a long time ago the king went forth to war and took you with him? I also went with you," said the wicked Manthara. "He was sorely wounded and would have died if you had not skillfully tended him and brought him back to life. In gratitude he offered you two boons and you said that you did not desire them then but would claim them when you needed them. You need them now, O Queen. For the first boon ask that Bhárata be made regent, and for the second that Rama be banished to the woods for fourteen years! During those years the people will forget him and will love Bhárata best of all, and even when Rama returns they will want your son to keep the throne. The king cannot refuse you; therefore act quickly, O lovely one!"

"How can I ask the king for two such boons?" asked her mistress.

"Go to the anger chamber at once," answered Manthara. "Loose your hair, cast off your jewels, lie down on the bare ground in your poorest raiment. When the king enters do not look up or speak, but lie there weeping, for he cannot bear your tears. He will offer you gold and jewels; refuse them and accept nothing but these two boons. Bind him with promises and use all the power of your beauty, O mistress, for your son's sake!"

The queen, possessed now by the evil design of her servant, followed Manthara as a chick follows its mother. In every queen's apartment there was a small, bare room where she could retire if she had been injured or if she desired something that was hard to grant. There the queen entered and flung her pearl necklace and all her other jewels and her garland of sweet, fresh flowers on the floor till it looked like the sky glittering with stars. Then she lay face down on the bare ground, loosing her beautiful hair and looking like a young doe struck down by the hunter.

The Banishment of Rama

After the king had dismissed Rama he went to the inner apartments, eager to tell the good news to his queens. He went first to the dwelling of his youngest and most beautiful queen, Kaikeyi, whom he loved dearly. He passed happily through the garden, where peacocks displayed their splendid tails and parrots screamed from the blossoming trees, and entered the room where the queen usually rested on her couch, awaiting his coming at the end of the day. But she was not there, and when he questioned a maidservant, she answered fearfully, "O Sire, she has entered the anger chamber."

The king's heart sank. He went into the small room and saw her lying on the ground like a broken garland or a nymph fallen from heaven.

"O lovely one, why are you displeased?" he asked. "Has anyone insulted you? Are you ill? I have skillful doctors who will restore you in an instant to health. Tell me what troubles you, for you have only to speak, and I will do whatever you wish, even at the cost of my life."

"I am not ill nor has anyone insulted me," answered the queen, still lying face downward. "I have one desire, which you can satisfy. If you are willing to do so, then give me your solemn promise, and I will tell you what it is."

The king sat down beside her and raised her body so that her head lay on his lap.

"You know that no one is dearer to me than you, except my son Rama," he said tenderly. "I swear to you by Rama, without whom I cannot live, that I will do whatever you ask of me."

Now the queen knew that she had him in her power, because he could never break a promise that he gave in the name of Rama.

"You remember, O King, that a long time ago you granted me two boons, after I had saved your life when you were sorely wounded in battle. I claim them now. O sun and moon," she cried, "O day and night, O gods and spirits, be witness now to the boons granted to me by this great king who has never broken his word!

"The first is that my son Bhárata be proclaimed your regent and heir. The second is that Rama be banished to the forest for fourteen years, taking a hermit's vows, so that Bhárata may rule undisturbed. This is the desire that you have promised to fulfill, O King."

The king's heart was pierced by these words as if they had been sharp arrows. He could not utter a word; he was like a quail when the hawk swoops upon it in a wood. He thought to himself, "Am I dreaming? Have I lost my mind or am I possessed by some evil spirit?" Then he came to himself and looked at Kaikeyi as if his glance could burn her to ashes.

"O wicked one, O destroyer of my house!" he cried. "How dare you demand the exile of Rama, who is the friend of all the world, whom all the people love for his generosity and purity, who is the protector of every living being? For what fault should he be banished? What harm has he or have I ever done to you that you should ask this thing? He has always treated you as he does his own mother, and you have often told me that you loved him as your own son. Bhárata is as virtuous as his brother; do you think that he will approve the banishment of Rama or that he will accept the throne while his elder brother lives? What evil spirit possesses you that you ask for such a boon?"

"If you repent of granting me those two boons, no one will call you just or righteous," she said. "When you are asked to make a promise, what will you say? That you broke your word to her who saved your life? Not only man is bound by his word; even the ocean, whose boundaries are fixed, does not pass beyond them when its tide is high at the time of the full moon. Truth is the crown of righteousness, O King. If you withdraw your pledge I shall drink poison before your eyes. Nothing will satisfy me save those two boons."

"Is it just or righteous to send my dear and truthful son into the forest?" he asked. "What will the kings and elders of the people say when they hear that at your behest I have changed my mind and banished my sinless son instead of crowning him? They will say that I am old and childish and deluded by a woman; the whole world will despise me. The people of my own city will hate me, for they love and honor Rama above all men. What can I say to his mother and to Sita? How can I give that pitiless message to him who has never spoken a harsh word to anyone?"

Then he pleaded with her: "O child, O giver of delight, I am old and my end is near. I beg of you to show mercy and to take back the words that you have spoken, and the wide world shall be yours. See, I lay my head upon your feet; be gracious to me and do not break my heart."

He fell at her feet and remained there speechless. When he recovered he begged her again and again to take back her deadly words, but the more he entreated the harder her heart became.

"If you withdraw your pledge I shall end my life," she said coldly. "O great King, you must fulfill the promise made to me, for it can never be revoked."

"O sinful woman, O evil one," he cried, "at the time of our wedding I took your hand in mine beside the sacred flame, but today I cast you away. You are no longer my wife. I have held you in my arms as a child plays with a venomous snake; I have cherished you as a man carefully keeps a rope that is going to hang him. I shall not live if Rama goes away. Let the preparations for his coronation be used for my funeral rites. Then govern this kingdom with your son, O destroyer of the house of Koshala!"

"Why do you grieve so much, O King?" she asked. "Put my son upon the throne and send Rama into exile. Then you will have done your duty."

The king realized that she would not change and that dire calamity was upon him and those he loved.

"I am caught in the net of destiny," he murmured. "I cannot understand what has happened. O starry night, do not pass away! O kindly night, have pity on me and forbid the dawn! How can I look upon the faces of the people, filled with joy because of the enthronement of Rama? O Rama, Rama!" he cried and sank down upon the floor like a felled tree.

The morning dawned; the high priest and his disciples came to the palace carrying the sacred water of the Ganges in a golden vessel, and various fragrant herbs, seeds, and jewels for the coronation. As he went through the streets they were being swept and watered and then strewn with flowers by happy people, talking and laughing with one another. Flags fluttered on the housetops and pots of incense and of sandalwood were being lighted. Shops were opened, filled with lovely merchandise, and stalls were set up where cool drinks and sweetmeats would be sold. Here and there companies of actors and dancers entertained the people, singing sweetly and playing their instruments. All were busy and full of joy.

When he arrived at the palace, the high priest found a crowd of Brahmans, warriors, and the chief merchants waiting in the court; musicians were chanting the praises of the king and of Rama; the sun was rising, but there was no word or movement from within. The priest met the king's trusted friend and charioteer, Sumantra, and asked him to tell the king that Rama must be crowned with all haste while the favorable star was at the zenith. Therefore Sumantra sought out the king and was surprised to find him in Queen Kaikeyi's rooms, his garments in disarray and his face distraught.

"Awake, O great King!" cried Sumantra. "Rejoice the hearts of the people by your presence! Don your royal robes and your most precious jewels, for the night is past and the joyful day is come when Rama will be crowned."

"Speak no more, Sumantra," said the king feebly, with bowed head. "Tell them to stop their music, for I cannot bear it."

Sumantra stepped back, amazed at these words, and the queen said to him, coolly, "The king was so happy that he did not sleep this night, so he is now tired. Go, Sumantra, and bring Prince Rama hither. His father wishes to see him."

The charioteer, wondering why the queen should wish to summon Rama, went to the prince's palace. His courts, too, were filled with priests and warriors, with yoked chariots whose handsome horses were eager to be off, and the great elephant on which he was to ride after his coronation. He found Rama, dressed in splendid robes and jewels, with Sita, as beautiful as the full moon, beside him. They had risen before dawn and had their palace cleaned and decorated. Poets and singers had delighted them by reciting the great deeds of Rama's ancestors and the glories of his dynasty. They said their morning prayers and worshiped the sun as it rose; then they dressed in their royal robes and jewels and awaited the summons of the king.

As soon as Sumantra gave him his father's message, Rama rose, bidding Sita await him there, and mounted the royal chariot, while his friends acclaimed him. Lákshmana was in the courtyard and mounted also, standing behind his brother. Sumantra urged the horses on and drove briskly through the gay, perfumed streets, surrounded by happy crowds who cheered and blessed them, while women threw flowers before them from the balconies. "O delight of your mother, how happy she will be today to see you crowned!" they cried. "Most fortunate of all women is the Princess Sita, who is so dear to you!" All along the way he heard words of praise and joy and when he entered the palace the multitude awaited his return as the ocean awaits the full moon.

Rama went into the inner rooms of the palace, followed by Lákshmana, and found his father, pale and unkempt, seated beside Kaikeyi. Fear struck at his heart as he beheld the king's misery; nevertheless he saluted them both with joined palms and waited for his father to speak. But the king, his voice choked with sorrow, could say only, "O Rama, Rama," and nothing more.

"Why is my father not happy to see me today?" asked

Rama and Lákshmana before the King

Rama, turning to the queen. "Have I displeased him? Why is he so pale and distressed? Answer me truly, O Queen, I beg of you."

"The king is not angry with you nor is he ill, O Rama," answered the queen, "but there is something that he fears to tell you because it is unpleasant and he loves you dearly. Long ago he granted me two boons which you must fulfill. Now he repents of them, like one who cares not for virtue. Have a care, Rama, lest the king abandon truth for love of you."

"For shame, Mother, to speak thus to me," answered Rama. "I am willing to do anything my father wishes me to do, even to casting myself into the fire or into the sea. Tell me now what he has promised; I vow that I will fulfill it. Rest assured; I do not break my word."

"The two boons I have asked of him, O virtuous one, are these," said the queen. "The first is that Bhárata be crowned regent instead of you, and the second is that you go into the forest for twice seven years, wearing a hermit's dress, living on fruits and roots, so that the earth may be ruled by your brother. It is for this that the king is distraught and cannot look at you. O Rama, obey him and fulfill his vow to me!"

That slayer of foes, hearing the queen's words, keen as the pangs of death, was in no way moved by them. He answered, "It shall be as you say! I shall honor my father's promise and leave at once for the forest to live a hermit's life for fourteen years. Therefore rejoice, O Queen! Send messengers on swift horses to summon my brother Bhárata from his grandsire's court and let him be

crowned! But why does my father not lay his commands
on me himself? Why does he sit with bowed head,
shedding tears? How much more would I do for him to
preserve his honor!"

"The king is overcome with shame and dares not ask
you to go," said the cruel queen. "Therefore go at once,
O Rama, for he will neither bathe nor eat until you have
departed."

The king cried out, "O woe, woe!" and fell back
fainting, on the couch. Rama lifted him up and then
made obeisance to him, touching his forehead to his
father's feet. He bowed low to the queen and took his
leave.

"I go to say farewell to my mother and to comfort my
Sita," he said to Kaikeyi. "Let Bhárata rule the kingdom
justly and serve our father faithfully."

With a serene and cheerful face, Rama came out into
the court where his friends and his father's priests and
ministers stood waiting. Lákshmana, his eyes filled with
tears and his heart with fury, followed him. Rama told
them what had happened and bade them farewell affec-
tionately, leaving them dumbfounded. Then he went on
to his own mother's rooms.

The queen had spent the whole night in prayer for
her son, and when he entered she was pouring a libation
on the sacred fire of her home. She went to him joyfully,
embracing and blessing him and offering him sweetmeats, which he merely touched, not taking any.

"O Mother, you have not heard of the misfortune that
has come to us," he said. "This is a season of sorrow for

you and for Sita and Lákshmana. Kaikeyi has claimed
two boons that the king promised her long ago. Now she
has forced my father to give the throne to Bhárata, while
I must go to the forest for fourteen years, dressed in
deerskins and eating fruit and roots and honey. I have
come to ask your permission to depart at once."

His mother's joy was turned in a moment to despair.

"O my son," she cried, "if I had never had a child I
should be spared this sorrow. How can I live, even for a
day, without seeing you? Why should you abandon me
at the unjust behest of my rival, your father's favorite
queen, who has bewitched him? You have a duty to me
as well as to him. If you go to the forest I shall surely die.
I forbid you to go, my son!"

Then Lákshmana spoke, breathing hard like an angry
snake, "O Rama, take over this kingdom before the
people have heard these evil tidings! I will stand beside
you, and who can oppose us, armed with our bows and
swords? How can the king dare to give the kingdom to
Bhárata while his eldest son still lives? He is old and
feeble and has been enslaved by a woman. If he opposes
you, I will slay even him; all your enemies shall fall
before me like clouds split by lightning. O my brother,
why must you submit to the will of a wicked woman?
What virtue or justice is there in my father's commands?
What valor is there in obeying them?"

"I know your love for me and I know your bravery
and your prowess; none can stand against you," answered
Rama. "But my bravery consists in obeying my father's
commands and fulfilling the vow he made to the queen.

The king is our ruler and our father; he is an old man; for all these reasons I must obey him. I am doing no new thing; many men in our royal line have sacrificed their very lives in obedience to their father's wishes. I walk in the path of my ancestors and of virtue. I cannot sacrifice duty for the sake of a kingdom."

He went to Lákshmana and wiped the tears from his brother's eyes. "Give up grief and anger, O dear one, and arm yourself with patience," he said. "Prepare now for my departure as willingly as you prepared for my coronation. This is the work of destiny. What man cannot understand must be the will of the gods. If it were not so, how could Kaikeyi, the daughter of a king, who has always looked upon me as her own son, speak such cruel and pitiless words today in the king's presence? When moved by destiny, people do not know what they say.

"O Mother, my father is sorely distressed by these boons that he has granted. When I am gone, do not let him be overcome by this great grief. For my sake, serve him well so that he may be alive when I return. Do not fear, I shall return after fourteen years when I have fulfilled my vow. Now grant me your permission to go, and pray for me in my absence."

"Alas, my child, I have no power to hold you back," said his mother, seeing that nothing would change his decision. "Enter the forest, then, in peace, and may happiness attend you! When you return, I shall know joy again." She called upon all the gods, the sun and the moon, the earth, the forests and rivers and all that inhabit them, to protect and bless him. He knelt and bent his head to her feet and left her.

He went on to his own palace to say the hardest farewell of all, to Sita. He passed serenely through the crowds of his sorrowing friends and followers, but as he came to Sita's rooms, his heart was stricken at the thought of leaving her, and he entered with his head bowed.

Sita rose, anxious and fearful. "What is this, my lord? This is the time of your coronation. Why are you here? What has happened that you look so distressesd?"

Rama told her the evil news, saying at last, "When I enter the forest, O dear one, remain here with a quiet heart. My father and my mother are both grieving because of my exile; comfort and serve them while I am away and obey our brother Bhárata when he is king, for he will protect you and care for you."

"O son of a great king, O Rama, how can you say such things?" she answered proudly. "Why, I could laugh at you, my lord. Do you not know that a wife is a part of her husband and shares all his fortunes? If you must go into exile and live in the forest, it is my right to go with you. I will walk before you, clearing the thorns and the sharp grass from your path. I will live with you in the forest as happily as in our own palace, wandering through the honey-scented woods according to the ancient spiritual custom, free from all worldly desire. My royal father taught me all the duties of a wife; is there any fault in me that would condemn me to stay here without you? Take me with you, O lord of my life! I shall not be a burden to you."

"Life in the forest is hard, my delicate princess," said Rama. "Do not think of sharing my exile. The rivers that rush down from the mountains are hard to cross; wild beasts roam about and their roaring will frighten you; marshes and rivers are full of crocodiles, and you hear the harsh cries of waterfowl; the way is barred with briars and sharp grass and fallen trees. Great storms visit the forest, and what will shelter you? When you are tired, there are no soft pillows or silken couches; you must sleep on the bare ground, your bed the fallen leaves; there is nothing to eat but fruit and berries and roots and what I can kill by hunting. Life is hard in the forest, my Sita; do not go with me but stay here in our home."

"All these hardships will be changed into joys if I am with you, my lord," said Sita. "If you can protect a kingdom with all its people, can you not protect one woman, O mighty hero? Journeying in the forest with you will not tire me; it will be like walking in the garden. The thorny briars will be as soft as deerskin. I shall share with you a couch of grass as gladly as I would a bed of silken down, and any food you bring me will be like the food of the gods. O what joy to be together in the forest! I fear nothing when I am near you, but I would rather die than remain here without you!"

Then Rama took her in his arms, "I advised you to stay here, O beautiful one, because I did not fully know your mind. But now, seeing your fixed resolve, my heart is filled with joy. Come with me, then, and help me to fulfill my duty. O Sita, let us prepare at once to go into exile, for I wish to leave today. Let us give all that we own to the Brahmans, to the old and the ill and to our servants, and then we shall go together, for I should not want to enter even heaven without you."

Lákshmana entered at this moment, his face still dark with grief and anger, and heard what Sita and his brother said. "If you are resolved to go to the forest, I will go with you and serve you," he said. "I shall go before you and clear the way, armed with my bow and carrying a spade and basket."

"You are as dear to me as my life, O Lákshmana," answered his brother, "but if you go, who will care for your mother and for mine? They will be unhappy with both of us gone, and Kaikeyi will not be kind to them."

"Bhárata will protect and cherish them," said Láksh-mana. "My mother still has Shátrughna, and those three will see to it that your noble mother comes to no harm. Let me go with you; sleeping and waking, I will serve you."

"Ask, then, the permission of your mother," said Rama joyfully, "and of your wife, Sita's sister, to go with us. Bring the great bows given by the gods to King Jánaka; bring our impenetrable armor and the two swords that Sita's father gave us when we were married. Then help me to give away all my wealth, O faithful one!"

5

The Way to the Forest

When Lákshmana returned with the weapons and armor, Rama summoned the Brahmans of the city and gave away all his wealth, pouring coins and jewels into their hands, while Sita gave her lovely robes and jewels to their wives. Cows and horses, elephants and chariots were given to his teachers, his fellow students, and his friends. Their servants were helping them, weeping; to each one Rama gave enough to keep him the rest of his life and said to them all, "Take care of this palace of mine until we return from the forest." Even more wealth was left over, and that was sent to the ill and the aged of the city.

There was one old priest who lived in great poverty with his wife and children. His wife said to him, "Hurry to Prince Rama's palace, for I have heard that he is giving

54

away all his wealth." The old man put on his rags, and leaning on his staff, hastened to the city and came to where Rama stood, surrounded by many people.

"I am a poor man with many children, great prince. Have pity on me!" he said.

Rama answered, half in joke, "I still have many cattle. Stand still and throw your staff as far as you can, and I will give you as many cows as can fill the space between you and the staff where it has fallen."

The old man bound his rags about him, twirled his staff and flung it with all his might. It flew through the air and sailed across the river to the opposite bank where many cows and bulls were grazing. Rama laughed and ordered all the cattle to be given to him, and the old priest went home delighted, driving his herd before him.

When all was done, Rama with his brother and Sita went on foot to take leave of their father, their servants following them carrying the great weapons.

Many people, sad and silent, watched them from the streets and the housetops. "Behold Lord Rama, who used to ride at the head of his army, followed now by a few servants." "The beautiful Sita, whom even the winds could not touch, now walks in the streets beheld by all the crowd." "Ah, what a prince! He did not rejoice at his coronation nor does he weep at his exile; pain and pleasure are the same to him. He is already a sage, although so young." "Surely the king is possessed by an evil spirit to send such a son into exile." They heard such words as these spoken by the people in the streets, but they walked on with serene faces, looking ahead.

When they came into the king's presence they found him overwhelmed by despair, his old age having suddenly come upon him; he was unable at first to speak a word. Then, for the first time, he looked into his son's face and said, "I have been deceived by Kaikeyi, because of a promise. O Rama, put me aside and seize the kingdom by force!"

But Rama answered him humbly, "May you rule the earth for many more years, O lord of men! I must go to the forest, since we both honor the truth, and in fourteen years I shall return to serve you again. Now give me your permission to go and grant also that Lákshmana and Sita go with me, since they are resolved, against my advice, to do so."

"O child, none can divert you from the path of truth," said the king. "I am tied by the rope of my own vow; I am caught in the net of destiny and I cannot forbid you. Go in peace and enter the forest and may no danger or hardship ever visit you there. Stay but one night more with your mother and me and set out in the morning early."

"If I stay for this night, what of tomorrow?" said Rama. "I wish to leave at once. O Father, do not grieve; I do not desire wealth or kingdom or pleasure; I shall be happy in the forest. All I wish is to carry out your commands and to uphold your honor. I shall return when the time is fulfilled. Bring me a hermit's dress and let us start at once."

The wicked queen, hearing these words, rose and brought three robes, woven of the coarse fiber of trees, and deerskins, such as hermits wear. She offered them to Rama, saying shamelessly, "Then put these on!"

Rama and Lákshmana laid aside their rich apparel, stepped from their jeweled sandals and put on the rough robes, throwing the deerskins over their shoulders. Standing barefoot and unadorned in the royal hall, they looked like the twin Ashvins, the Gods of Dawn and Twilight. Sita, dressed in a soft-hued silken sari, looked at the dress offered to her as a doe looks at a snare. She turned to Rama and asked piteously, "How does one wear these robes?"

He started to help her, but the king's high priest rose in anger and said sternly to the queen, "You are dead to all decency and good sense, O evil-minded one, O destroyer of your husband's dynasty! You asked only for the exile of Rama. Sita chooses to go with him. Let her be richly clad and adorned and let her go to the forest in a royal chariot!"

The king, his voice weak and choked with sorrow, ordered Sumantra to yoke the finest horses to his chariot and then said to his treasurer, "Bring costly robes and jewels that will serve the princess for fourteen years!"

When all the farewells were said, Rama, Sita, and Lákshmana, with joined palms, walked three times round the king, keeping him on their right, even as the sun shines on the earth; even as the sun bestows every blessing and protects from evil and darkness, so with reverence, they blessed him as they departed. Then they mounted the chariot with cheerful hearts, and Sumantra drove them from the palace to the great gate.

The people of the city were as if crazed by grief. Young and old ran after the chariot, crying to Sumantra, "Drive slowly, O charioteer, so that we may see the face of Rama a little longer! Faithful is the princess Sita who follows her lord as his shadow. Noble is his brother who shares his misfortune. How can we live without them?"

Rama looked back and saw that his father and mother had come out of the palace and were gazing after the chariot, their arms outstretched. He could not bear the sight and said, "Drive faster, O Sumantra!" while the people cried, "Slower! Slower, O charioteer!" The dust raised by the wheels of the chariot was laid by the people's tears.

After they had passed the gate many people still followed, running beside the chariot, weeping and begging Rama to return. "O people of Ayodhya," he said, "for my sake bestow the love and honor that you show to me—yes, and more—upon my brother Bhárata. He is wise and gentle and courageous and will rule you well. Do not cause him any distress when I am in the forest, and if you wish to please me, obey my father, who has given him the throne."

But the people still followed him, as if drawn by a cord. "O swift and excellent steeds, do not carry Rama from us into the forest!" they cried. "See, even the trees try to follow and bend their branches to the ground, but they are held back by their strong roots. Have pity on them and on us!"

Rama looked back and saw that many Brahmans and old people were still trying to keep up with the chariot;

so he told Sumantra to stop, and he and Lákshmana and Sita walked slowly ahead, in order not to tire those who were on foot. As the sun set, a river barred their way, and they decided to spend the night on its bank. Sumantra loosed the horses and let them roll on the ground while he gathered grass for them to eat. Rama, Sita, and Lákshmana drank only some water and fasted; and when darkness came, all that company lay down to rest, fasting, on the ground. Lákshmana and Sumantra gathered young leaves and made a bed for Rama and Sita, who were soon peacefully asleep; but the other two stayed awake all that night, keeping watch and talking quietly to one another of all that had occurred that day.

At dawn Rama awoke and, seeing the people lying asleep, said to Lákshmana, "The people who are sleeping here are determined to bring us back to Ayodhya. Let us leave before they wake so that they may not suffer or tire themselves further. If they find us gone they will return home."

Lákshmana agreed, and Rama said to Sumantra, "Yoke the horses quietly and let us drive swiftly and silently away, so that the people do not see us go."

They crossed the river at a shallow ford and drove along a rough path overgrown with briars where the mark of the wheels could not be seen; then they came out upon a pleasant road where they could travel freely, and they drove on swiftly toward the southern border of Koshala. As they went they looked with joy on the prosperous towns, on the fine highways, the fields full of grazing cattle, the pools of water and groves of trees that bespoke the wise rule of the king. When they had crossed the southern boundary, Rama turned his face toward Ayodhya and with joined palms addressed it, "O Ayodhya, loveliest of cities, I take my leave of you and of the gods who dwell in you and protect you. When the time of my vow is fulfilled, I shall come back from the forest and behold you and my parents again."

After they had passed the boundary of the kingdom they came to the sacred river Ganges, on whose banks holy men gather to perfect their lives, to whose waters the celestial nymphs and even the gods come to play and bathe. Its waves rippled with the sound of laughter; white lotuses blossomed in its pools, where swans and ducks abounded, while cranes stood beside its high banks or on its shelving sands.

Beholding that mighty river, beautiful as a woman adorned with jewels, Rama said, "Let us stop here and rest, O kind charioteer. We shall find shelter under that great fig tree whose wide branches and broad leaves will protect us." They unyoked the horses and offered homage to the river and then sat at the foot of the tree, looking across at the forest that was to be their home.

While they rested there the king of the small country that bordered the river came with his ministers to welcome them, for he had heard of their exile. He was a ferryman named Guha, but he possessed territory and an army and was called the king of watermen. He was sorrowful when he saw Rama clad in a hermit's dress, and said, "O prince, I am your servant. Let my small

kingdom be to you as Ayodhya and rule it as if it were
your own, for we are all obedient to you. Pray accept this
food that I have brought, cooked with honey and spices,
these soft beds, and fodder for your horses."

"You have come here on foot to welcome us, O Guha,
and I am much honored by you," answered Rama. "But
I have taken a hermit's vow and may eat nothing but
fruit and roots and what we may bring down with our
arrows. We may not linger in your kingdom, for tomorrow we must cross the river and enter the forest. I gladly
accept fodder for the horses, for they are tired, and my
father loves them. This and your kind welcome are
enough hospitality."

Guha spent the night with them under the fig tree,
and in the morning before sunrise, when the birds were
singing, he ordered his ferrymen to bring a sturdy boat.
They took the two brothers' great weapons and the light
chest containing Sita's robes and jewels and placed them
in the boat, for the chariot could go no farther.

Sumantra came to Rama with joined palms and said,
"What more can I do for you, O lion among men?"

"Return to the king, O good Sumantra, and serve him
well so that he does not sink under the weight of sorrow," said Rama. "Tell him that Sita and Lákshmana
and I have entered the forest and are not troubled; that
fourteen years will soon pass, and that we shall see him
again. Give the same message to our mothers, bowing
to their feet, and when Bhárata returns, tell him for me
to give them all the same love and honor that he gives
the king."

Then Sumantra wept and said, "How can I return without you, O sinless one? When the chariot returns empty the heart of the city will be broken in two. Let me stay with you! The horses and the chariot may be useful to you and I will serve you in any way I can. My greatest desire is to drive you back to Ayodhya when the fourteen years are over. Give me leave, my lord, I beg of you!"

"I know your devotion, O Sumantra, but I will tell you why I wish you to return," said Rama. "When Queen Kaikeyi sees you, she will know that I have entered the forest, and she will leave my father in peace. Bhárata also will know that I shall be away for fourteen years and that he must govern the kingdom. I wish my father and my mothers to receive the messages that I have sent them. Therefore, to please me, return quickly to the city."

Then he and Sita and Lákshmana took leave of Sumantra and Guha and entered the boat, which was driven swiftly across the current by the strong arms of the oarsmen. In midstream Sita, delighted by the beauty of the great river, joined her hands together and worshiped it, saying, "O blessed Ganges, I bow down and adore you. Protect, I pray you, this noble prince who obeys his father's commands. When he returns safely and occupies his throne, I will give you a thousand cows. When I return to Ayodhya I will offer you a sacrifice of a hundred jars of wine and rice. O goddess, grant that Rama and Lákshmana, free of sin, return again to their kingdom!"

When they reached the farther bank, the forest received them and they found a path leading into it. "This is our first day in the wilderness by ourselves," said Rama to his brother. "We must protect Sita carefully from now on. Do you go first to search out the way, let Sita follow you, and I will come last to defend you both. So far the daughter of Jánaka has not tried her strength, but today she will have to bear the hardships of a hermit's life. Until we find a home, only one of us shall sleep at night."

They went deep into the woods, finding fruit and berries to quench their hunger and clear brooks to refresh them. Then Lákshmana hunted a deer and they roasted its flesh over a flame which they kindled by rubbing together two sticks of wood. As darkness came they found a sheltering tree and made their beds of grasses and the tender leaves of spring. Instead of soft couches with silken covers only these leaves were between them and the hard ground; instead of the gleam of polished and finely wrought lamps of gold and silver, the bright stars shone far off between the branches; instead of a palace filled with people who loved and served them, the nearby dwellings of their father, mothers, and brothers and the peaceful city they loved so well, the black and lonely forest surrounded them, where night birds cried and fluttered, and far off they heard the howls of beasts that hunt their prey by night.

They could not sleep at first for the strangeness and the solitude, and they talked long together, wondering what was happening in Ayodhya and what Bhárata would do when he heard of their exile and his coming coronation. And Rama, now that he was alone with the two whom he loved best, thinking of his parents' sorrow and of all that he had lost, laid aside the control that he had put upon himself for so long, and wept bitterly.

The next morning the sun rose in a cloudless sky, and they went on toward the place where the river Jumna runs into the Ganges. For Sita's sake they rested often under flowering trees, on soft grasses, and she delighted in the many singing birds, in the monkeys peering at them from the treetops or swinging gracefully among the branches, in the herds of deer and delicate antelopes who wandered freely there, for no man hurt them.

Toward the end of the day they saw smoke, as blue as a pigeon's neck, rising through the trees, and went toward it. They found a hermitage where a mighty saint dwelt who welcomed them as they bowed reverently before him and told him their names. He offered them water to wash their feet, and a hermit's food.

"I know that you have been banished without cause," he said. "Stay here and live in peace in this holy place where the two great rivers meet."

"Your hermitage, O blessed one, is too close to the abode of men," answered Rama. "I fear that people would seek us out if we remained here. Tell us of a lonelier place where we may live in peace."

The hermit told them that a beautiful mountain, named Chitrakuta, lay but ten miles away, that it was purified by the presence of many holy men, and that animals and birds lived freely there, undisturbed by anyone. So they slept that night at the hermitage, and neither brother needed to stay awake to watch over Sita.

Then, with the blessing of the sage, they went on to the mountain, which lay on the far side of the Jumna. The two brothers gathered wood and built a raft, tying the logs together with long vines, and filled the cracks with grass and leaves. Lákshmana spread young branches to make a seat for Sita, and she, clinging to Rama's hand, took her place while the brothers laid their belongings on the floor of the raft. Again she prayed to the river and offered it sacrifices when they should all return.

They found the mountainside even more beautiful than the hermit had said it was, and saw with wonder and delight, trees and blossoms, birds and beasts that they had never known before. Lákshmana climbed high into the trees to bring flowers to Sita, who wove them into garlands; he gathered a honeycomb as large as a waterpot that hung from a branch and fruits that also clustered there.

Everywhere the birds sang and peacocks spread their splendid tails before their modest hens. A clear river flowed nearby, and this mountain seemed the perfect place for their hermitage. They found a level field bordered with trees and chose that for their dwelling place.

Rama and Lákshmana took their axes, cut young trees and drove them into the ground in the form of a square; then they wove flexible branches between the posts and raised a roof thatched thickly with broad leaves; soft grasses made the floor. Lastly they built altars on the

four sides, and after they had bathed in the river, offered
sacrifices of fruit and flowers to the gods and repeated
the Vedic prayers. When they entered the hut, sheltered
from wind, rain, and sun, their hearts were filled with
joy.

"How beautiful it is here!" said Rama. "O Sita, I
could live here with you and Lákshmana for countless
years and feel no grief or anxiety. How splendid are these
peaks that reach to the skies and gleam with veins of
gold and jewels! When the wind stirs the trees the hills
seem to dance and the flowers that it scatters are like
offerings to this lovely river on which they fall. There
are shallows here where we can bathe and play as you
used to play with your maidens at home, my dear one,
pelting them with flowers and with splashes of water.
Surely we shall be happy here and never miss the com-
forts of Ayodhya."

6

Bharata's Return

Sumantra watched the three leave the boat on the opposite shore of the river and followed them with his eyes until they were lost to sight. Then he yoked his unwilling horses, which also gazed after Rama, the tears falling from their eyes. He bade farewell to Guha and drove back the way that he had come, reaching Ayodhya on the evening of the third day.

The city was stricken and silent. No children played in the streets nor was there any sound of music or of laughter. The shops were closed and the markets empty; the birds sat motionless on the trees, and in the houses no lamp was lighted. The once happy city was like an emptied pool where water jars lie on the parched earth; like a tavern deserted by revelers, the wine spilled and

67

fragments of glass lying on the bare floor; like a meteor that falls dead upon the earth, its flame extinguished.

Sumantra went to the palace and entered the inner apartments, asking for the king. He found him in the rooms of Rama's mother, lying old and feeble on a couch, attended by his two queens, for he would have nothing to do with the wicked one who had betrayed him. Sumantra gave Rama's message to the king and the queens. The old man received it in silence, but Queen Kaushalya, the mother of Rama, wept anew as she asked Sumantra how he had left them, how they looked and where they slept, and how the tender Sita bore the hardships of her life.

"Do not grieve or be anxious for them, O Queen," said the charioteer. "They will live happily in the forest. Prince Lákshmana will serve his brother devotedly, and the princess will be as happy there as in her own home. Indeed Ayodhya would be a wilderness to her without Rama and the forest will be a pleasure garden, since she is with him. Her beauty is not marred by the fatigue of the journey, by the winds or by the heat of the sun. She has not put off her jewels, but walks the forest paths with tinkling anklets and feet as fresh as lotus petals. There is no need to grieve for these three. The willing exile of your son, to fulfill his father's vow, will be remembered by the whole world as long as the sun and moon abide in the heavens."

But the king could not be comforted. When night came he lay awake, wondering again why this great misfortune had come to pass. Then he remembered a grievous sin that he had committed, though unwittingly, in his youth. He called to his queen, "Draw near and touch me, O Kaushalya, for I cannot see you. A man must gather the fruit of all that he does whether it is good or evil. Let me tell you how I have destroyed my own happiness by a deed which I did long ago out of ignorance.

"When I was young, before I was king, I prided myself on my skill in archery. I learned to aim my arrows in the dark, following a sound. One night I went to the river bank to hunt, at a place where elephants, tigers, and buffaloes came to drink. I heard the sound of water being taken up and shot a poisoned arrow toward the sound, thinking an elephant had come there. But, alas, I heard a human voice cry out, 'Who has slain me? I have no enemies in the world and live a hermit's life here in the woods. What will my parents do when I am dead? Alas, we are all slain by a single arrow.'

"I went to him and found a youth lying mortally wounded on the ground. 'O warrior,' he said, 'what harm have I done to you that you have killed me while I fetched water for my parents? They are old and blind and cannot live without me. Go quickly now, by the path behind you, to my father's hut and try to make your peace with him, lest he curse you or burn you to ashes with his anger!'

"With those words he gave up his life. I filled the pitcher that had fallen from his hands and followed the path to his parents' hermitage, where with anguish I told them what I had unwittingly done. They asked me to lead them to where their son's body lay, and when they

touched it they lamented sorely for him. Then the father said to me, 'If you had done this knowingly, I would
have burned you to ashes with my curse. Since you did
not, I will lay this lesser curse upon you: that you suffer
the same grief that you have caused me. The loss of your
son shall cause your own death.' Then the two gathered
wood and kindled a fire; they laid their son's body
upon it, and when it was burned they entered the fire
themselves and joined their only child. Now the curse
of that father has been fulfilled; I have lost my son and
I die."

Thus, overwhelmed by his grief, that mighty and
generous king at midnight gave up his life.

On the morning after the king's death his ministers
met together and the chief priest said, "The king is dead;
Lord Rama is in the forest with the mighty Lákshmana,
and Prince Bhárata, with Shátrughna, is in his grandfather's city, many miles away. We must send for him
immediately, since his father has promised the kingdom
to him. A land without a king falls into ruin: the farmers sow no grain; sons do not obey their fathers nor wives
their husbands. In a land without a king there is no
peace: thieves and brigands have their way, the rich are
not protected, and the cowherd, the shepherd, and the
farmer cannot sleep at ease with open doors. The holy
festivals are not held, nor do actors or the leaders of song
and dance find joy in such a land. For the king is a father to his people; he leads them in the path of virtue
and is their greatest benefactor."

He then summoned trusted messengers and bade them

go at once to fetch Bhárata and his brother. "Say to him that he is needed urgently in Ayodhya, but do not tell him that his father is dead or that Rama is exiled," he said to them. "Take fine robes and jewels for his grandfather, the king."

The messengers rode as swiftly as the horses were able to go, but still it took them nearly a week to reach the kingdom of Kekaya. There Bhárata asked after the welfare of the king, the queens, and his brothers, and the messengers answered, "All those who are dear to you are well, O lion among men. But summon your chariot, for you are needed at home."

Bhárata and Shátrughna asked their grandfather's permission to depart and gave him the gifts sent from Ayodhya. Then they had horses saddled and left the city, followed by elephants, camels, and carts bearing gifts from their grandfather. They were troubled by the urgent message they had received and outdistanced their escort, traveling through Panchala, crossing the Ganges at the great city of Hástina, until on the seventh day, with tired horses, they arrived at the gate of Ayodhya.

There they found the city sad and silent and their hearts were sick with dread. They entered the palace, where no one met them, and strode through the halls seeking the king. Finding him nowhere, they went to the apartments of Bhárata's mother, where their father often sat.

Queen Kaikeyi, happy to see her son after his long absence, rose and embraced him. He and Shátrughna made obeisance to her, touching her feet, and answered

her first questions as to their welfare. Then Bhárata
asked anxiously, "Tell me, Mother, why the city is so
sad and empty. Where is my father, whom I have come
so far to see?"

His mother told him of the king's death, and the two
princes mourned their father bitterly, for they loved and
honored him. "How fortunate my brothers were, who
were here when he died!" said Bhárata. "Where is
Rama? Now that he is king, he will be a second father
to me. Where are he and Lákshmana?"

Then his mother told him the whole story of the two
boons that she had demanded of the king: "When I
heard that Rama was to be crowned king, I asked your
father to banish him and to bestow the kingdom upon
you, and he did so because he had to keep his promise
to me. Then he died, since he could not bear to be separated from his eldest son. All this I brought about for
your sake, my child. Do not grieve; perform the funeral
rites for your noble father and accept the throne, for the
kingdom and the city are now without a ruler and depend on you for their very life!"

Bhárata rose, his eyes red with anger. "O sinful one, O
destroyer of the family, how did you ever think of such
a deed?" he cried. "Why have you slain my father and
banished Rama, who ever delights in virtue and who
loved you as his own mother? What have you gained
by such wickedness? Did you not know how much I love
and honor Rama? Did you believe that I would rule the
kingdom while he lived? It is the custom in our noble
house that the eldest brother rules and that the younger

ones obey him. You do not know the duty of a king or the rules of government, though you yourself were born of a royal house. You have cast the glory and the honor of this kingdom into the dust, and it is I who must bear the blame of your wickedness, for all men will despise me, and I am bereft of my father and of my two brothers.

"O cruel-hearted one, O traveler on the road to your own ruin, listen well to what I say! I will never fulfill your evil designs! I shall bring Rama back from the forest and serve him with my whole heart for the rest of my life!"

He left her, and the queen, seeing that she lost both her husband and her son, and that her plans had come to nothing, began to repent bitterly of what she had done.

The mother of Rama, Queen Kaushalya, heard the sound of Bhárata's lamentation and went forth from her rooms to find him. Bhárata and Shátrughna saw how pale and weak she was and wept as they bowed before her, touching her feet. In her sorrow she spoke bitter words, saying, "You wished to rule the kingdom, O Bhárata, and your cruel mother has fulfilled your desire and made you the sovereign of this great empire. But why must the pitiless queen send my son into exile? Let her banish me also! O Bhárata, take me to that place where Rama, that lion among men, lives like a hermit in a garment made of bark!"

"O Mother, you know how dearly I love Rama and that I am quite innocent of his exile," said Bhárata, pained by her hard words. "If I caused or agreed to the exile of Rama, may I forget the holy books and the tra-

ditions of our race! May I become the slave of the lowest
caste or beg my bread from door to door, clothed in
rags! May I receive the punishment of one who rebels
against a just king, of one who does not pay the wages
of those who labor for him, of one who strikes a cow,
who speaks evil of his teacher or betrays his friends! If
I ever had a secret wish to banish Rama, may I meet the
fate of one who eats good food but offers none to the
gods, to his ancestors, or his guests! May I fall as low
as one who abandons his hungry children, who turns
away from a faithful wife, as one who drinks the milk
of a cow whose calf is not yet weaned, or who sleeps at
sunrise or at sunset!

"If I have ever done anything but love and obey my
elder brother, whose countenance is as radiant as the sun
and the moon, may I not live to see his coronation!"

The queen was convinced of his innocence and embraced him tenderly, saying, "It is fortunate that your
heart and those of the twins are ever devoted to Rama.
Surely you will all enter the regions of the blest!"

Then Bhárata, finding himself unwillingly in Rama's
place, took up the duties of the eldest son. First of all
the funeral rites of the old king must be held. His body
had been embalmed until at least one of his sons could
be present; now it was clothed in royal garments and
carried on a litter to the bank of the river, where a pyre
of fragrant woods was raised. All the court, the three
queens, the priests, and many citizens followed the litter,
Bhárata and Shátrughna leading them. They stood beside the pyre while it blazed and consumed the king's

body; they poured libations upon it while the priests recited the holy verses. Then they returned to the city, and for ten days of mourning they slept on the bare ground.

One day when Bhárata and Shátrughna were talking together, the hunchback Manthara came to the door of the women's apartments. They had heard of the part she had played in their great misfortunes, but had not seen her. Now one of the palace guards seized her and brought her to them. "This is the sinful wretch who caused the death of the king and the exile of Lord Rama," he said. She was dressed in splendid garments and adorned with jewels and looked like a pet monkey. Shátrughna took her and shook her so hard that her jewels flew off in all directions and she shrieked with terror. He threw her down and dragged her into Kaikeyi's room, where he reviled them both with bitter words. Kaikeyi, too, was terrified and appealed to Bhárata, who said to his brother, "Women must never be slain or even hurt by us. If it were not so, what would I not have done to this queen, my mother? Rama would wish us to forgive this crippled woman; therefore set her free, O Shátrughna!" Manthara fell, trembling and weeping, at Kaikeyi's feet and the two brothers left them.

On the fourteenth day, after the king's ashes had been gathered and the last rites performed, the high priest summoned the two princes, the ministers and the counselors of the kingdom, and the leaders of the army, to the assembly hall. He said to Bhárata, "Today you are our lord, O mighty prince. The kingdom has no ruler, and your father left it to you. Your coronation has been prepared and everyone looks to you for protection and guidance. Therefore ascend the throne of your noble ancestors!"

"It is known to you, O sinless one, that in our royal house the throne is always inherited by the eldest son," answered Bhárata. "Therefore it is not right that you should ask this of me. The kingdom belongs to Rama and I also belong to him, since he is my elder brother. I never wished to rule and I knew nothing of what happened in my absence, since I was far away. My heart is filled with anguish because of my father's death and my brother's exile. Now I intend to bring him back to Ayodhya and to his rightful kingdom, while I go into exile for fourteen years in his place. I shall start at once for the forest and shall crown him there. Therefore let roads be made and rough places smoothed, so that the army may follow us and all of you, the queens, and the chiefs of the people may be present at his coronation!"

There was great joy at this announcement in the palace and among the citizens, who were happy for the first time in many sad weeks. All praised the faithfulness of Bhárata and rejoiced that Rama would soon be with them. The city was busy again as skilled mechanics, bridge builders, woodcutters, and all kinds of workmen streamed from the gates to prepare the way, while the streets were washed and decorated. The people laughed and talked again and heard the sound of drums and cymbals.

When all was ready, Bhárata and Shátrughna

mounted their chariot and set forth eagerly. Ministers and priests rode on horseback or in chariots; the great elephant that was to bear Rama back was richly caparisoned and decorated; the queens and their ladies traveled in curtained litters; the leaders of the army and the chief merchants of the city followed, and dozens of carts drawn by bullocks carried food and tents and other baggage. All went joyfully forward to bring Rama home again.

The road had been smoothed and widened all the way to the Ganges, where Sumantra had left the two princes and Sita, and there Bhárata set up his camp for the night.

Guha, the ferryman, had seen them coming and was frightened at the sight of warriors and such a large company. He called his ministers and followers together. "The flag of Koshala flies over the largest tent of this great army," he said. "It must be Prince Bhárata who comes here to find Rama. Perhaps he wishes to slay his elder brother in order to make his rule secure. Arm yourselves, my friends, and line the river bank; call all our boats together and let their crews be well armed! If Bhárata means no harm, we shall welcome him and ferry him across."

Then Guha went to meet Bhárata, carrying the usual offerings of food. Sumantra had told the prince that the ferryman was a good friend of Rama, and Bhárata welcomed him warmly. "Tell me, O King of watermen," he said, "how I can reach the dwelling place of my two brothers and Sita? I know that with your help they crossed the river at this place."

"Have no fear, great prince," said Guha. "My followers know the forest well; they will guide you, and I myself will go with you. But this great army frightens me. Do you seek Rama with any evil intent?"

"Do not think evil of me, my friend," answered Bhárata, whose heart was as pure as the unclouded sky. "I go to crown Lord Rama and bring him back from his exile; he is as dear to me as my father."

"O Bhárata, there is none equal to you in the world," said Guha joyfully. "Your fame will live forever, since for your brother's sake you give up an empire that has fallen into your hands through no act of your own."

They rested and spent the night on the bank of the river, and in the morning Guha gathered hundreds of boats and rafts together to take them across. There were only footpaths on the other side, and the great crowd of men and animals had to break their way through the forest, cutting down trees and leveling the ground, and the noise they made and the dust they raised frightened the animals and birds, who fled away on all sides.

Guha led Bhárata to the hermitage of that saint who had welcomed the three exiles on their second night in the forest. When they came near to it, Bhárata told the rest of the company to halt there, while he put off his weapons and his rich attire. Clad in a single garment, he approached the saint with the high priest and Shátrughna. The holy one welcomed them and refreshed them with forest fruits. Then he told them where Rama had gone and that they would surely find his dwelling on the side of the lovely mountain Chitrakuta.

Before they left, the queens came to take leave of the sage, and he asked Bhárata to present each one as she came forward to touch his feet. "Here is my father's chief queen, O holy one," said Bhárata, "weak with fasting and sorrow. She is the mother of Rama, that lion among men. And this one who is ever near her is the mother of those heroes Lákshmana and Shátrughna. O great sage, she who has brought about all our sorrow and caused the death of the king, the cruel Kaikeyi, is my mother."

But the holy one, who knew both the past and the future, looked upon Kaikeyi, who stood stricken with remorse, apart from the others, and said, "Do not reproach your mother, my son. The exile of Rama will bring about great good."

Then the whole great company set out joyfully for Chitrakuta.

Rama, Sita, and Lákshmana had become accustomed to their life in the forest and were very happy there. They bathed two or three times a day in the bright waters of the river, where cranes and wild geese stood in the shallows and where they gathered lotus blossoms and water lilies. They walked through the woods, finding cool caves and flowery clearings; they sought out the finest fruit trees—fig, mango, breadfruit, and banana—and gathered honey and berries for their food and for offerings to the gods. Sometimes the two brothers shot a deer or an antelope and used the soft skins to cover their beds and to make warm garments. Sometimes they speared fish in the river, broiling the sweet flesh over a fire they built on the sands.

One day they were sitting on a rock near their dwelling, eating venison that they had roasted. Suddenly a great noise disturbed the peace of the forest, and they saw a cloud of dust rising above the trees. Birds fled by with cries of fear, and a herd of deer leaped swiftly through the woods. Lákshmana climbed a tree and saw the vast company of Bhárata, with its horses and elephants, its chariots and litters.

"Put out the fire, brother, and arm yourself!" he called. "Let Sita enter the cave, for an army comes."

"Look at the flag and see whose army it is," answered Rama.

"I see a chariot with a white flag bearing the emblem of our own dynasty," cried Lákshmana angrily. "Bhárata has come to kill us both so that he may rule in peace. O Rama, let us arm ourselves, for surely there is no sin in slaying one who has wronged you. O mighty one, to-day I will let loose the anger that has been hidden in my heart and free the world of Kaikeyi and her son, and you shall rule the whole earth."

"What harm has Bhárata ever done us that you should speak so harshly of him?" Rama answered. "I am sure that when he returned and found us gone, he wished to come here to see us out of love and grief. I can see no other reason for his coming. If you speak thus because of the kingdom, O Lákshmana, I will ask him to give it to you. If I say to him, 'O Bhárata, give the kingdom to Lákshmana,' he will surely do it."

"I see the royal elephant," said Lákshmana, abashed by his brother's reproach. "Perhaps it is our father who has come to see us. But I do not see the white canopy that would be held above his head if he were there."

While they spoke, the noise had ceased, for Bhárata had seen the smoke of their fire and wished to meet Rama with only Shátrughna, Sumantra, and Guha. He followed a well-worn path and saw first a charming hut on whose walls hung bright shields and mighty bows and quivers of arrows; then he saw his beloved brother, clad in a hermit's dress, seated between Sita and Lákshmana.

Bhárata ran forward, speaking his brother's name, and knelt weeping at his feet. Shátrughna also bowed to Rama's feet and then to Sita's, and the four brothers embraced one another with unspeakable joy. Then Rama, looking at Bhárata, said, "I scarcely know you, dear brother, you look so thin and so careworn. What brings you here to the forest? Is the king, our father, well, or has grief ended his life?"

Bhárata told him of his father's death, and Rama grieved sorely, knowing that his own departure had been the cause of it. He and his brothers went to the river, and standing in it, filled the palms of their hands with its pure waters, and Rama said, "O mighty King, may this water offered today by your sons be yours forever in the realm of our ancestors." In the same way they offered to his spirit the fruit and berries of the forest.

Then the high priest, the ministers, the queens, and the citizens came forward and Rama greeted them all, touching the feet of the priests and the three queens, while his mother and Lákshmana's embraced their sons and Sita joyfully. Everyone felt as if the exiles had been away for years although, indeed, it had been only a few weeks.

When the joyful meeting was over, all those who had come sat down around the hut, looking at the two brothers who sat side by side; for they all longed to know what Bhárata would say to Rama and what the answer would be. For a time there was a deep silence; no one spoke and they felt at peace.

At last Bhárata said, "O mighty one, our father, the king, was forced by my mother to do a shameful thing, and he has died of grief in consequence. Although I am Kaikeyi's son I am your devoted follower and servant. I beg of you to let yourself be crowned today and to ascend the throne. The priests and ministers of the kingdom, the elders of the people, and my mother herself have come to entreat you. O best of men, you are the eldest son and should by right succeed our father. Accept the burden of kingship and fulfill our desire! The earth, ruled by you, will be as content as the winter night when the moon is full. I will put on a hermit's dress and take your place in the forest. O Rama, do not let us plead in vain!"

Bhárata, his eyes filled with tears, bowed his head to Rama's feet. His elder brother raised him and embraced him. "O Bhárata, how can a good and wise prince ask his elder brother to do wrong?" he said. "The father, the king, or the spiritual teacher can command us to do whatever he wills, and our duty is to obey. Our father commanded me to go to the forest and you to ascend the throne. How can we dare to disobey? Return to Ayodhya, O sinless one, and enjoy the kingdom my father has given you, while I remain here and enjoy what he has given me. I should not want to rule over the whole world in defiance of his will."

"Be gracious to me and listen to me, O Rama!" entreated his brother. "When I was far away my mother committed the sin that causes all my sorrow. I am born of a virtuous king and I know what is evil and what is good. It is said that a man loses his judgment as he draws near to death, and our father has proved this to be true. How else could a man who knew so well the laws of virtue do such a thing in order to please a woman? He acted also without consulting his advisors or the people. You are not bound by such a deed; you should rather hide it from the world and so defend the good name of the king.

"O Rama, it is your duty to save your father, my mother, and myself from the results of this deed which everyone condemns. It is your duty as a Kshatria to protect and rule your people. O noble one, listen to me! I am only a child, compared to you, in wisdom, in virtue, and in rank. How can I be king? With my head at your feet I entreat you to wash away the stain of my mother's guilt and to let us all rejoice at your coronation."

All those who were present praised Bhárata and added their entreaties to his. They admired the faithfulness of Rama and yet longed for his return.

"Two boons were granted by my father to your mother, O Bhárata," said Rama. "In order to uphold his honor and the truth of his word, I am willing to fulfill one of them and to live in the forest for twice seven years. Now it is for you to redeem the second boon: to return to Ayodhya and accept the throne. Be the king of men, my brother, and I will reign here over the animals of the forest. The royal canopy shall shelter you from the sun's heat, and the cool shadows of the trees shall give me shade. Shátrughna will attend you and Lákshmana will stay here with me. So shall we, the four sons of our noble father, guard his honor in the realm of truth."

Then the high priest spoke to him, reminding him that from the beginning, in the noble dynasty to which Rama belonged, the eldest son inherited the throne. "It is not right for you to break this sacred rule, my son," he said. "When a man is born he must obey his father, his mother, and his spiritual teacher. Parents give men their body, but the teacher gives them wisdom. I am your father's teacher and yours; hear my counsel and follow the path of virtue. Behold, here are your relatives, the learned priests, the warriors and merchants of the capital; here is your mother, whom you should obey. Do your duty to us all and yield to your brother's entreaty!"

"The good that parents do to their son cannot easily be repaid," Rama answered. "When he is a child they dress him in delicate clothes and give him tempting foods; they put him to rest and tenderly rub his body with oil and give him gentle counsel; they teach him what he needs for his welfare. I cannot set aside the commands of my father. The moon may lose its light and the Himalayas their snow, the ocean may overflow its bounds, but I shall not break the vow I made in his presence."

Bhárata said to Sumantra, "Bring some kusha grass, O charioteer, and make a seat for me here at the door of Lord Rama's hut. I will sit here and fast until he consents to return to Ayodhya."

"What wrong have I done you, dear brother, that you should sit thus before me?" asked Rama. "A man may do so to one who has wronged him, but it is not right for you to act so to me."

Bhárata turned to the citizens of Ayodhya who sat silent around him. "Why do you not also entreat Lord Rama?" he asked them.

"We cannot entreat him any more," answered one of them, "for his mind is made up."

Then Bhárata surrendered, falling at his brother's feet and crying, "O Rama, Rama!" He had brought royal raiment for the coronation; now he sent an attendant to fetch the sandals adorned with gold and jewels that were a part of that apparel. "Place your feet in these sandals, O blessed one," he said, "for they will be all that we have to support and protect us."

Rama put his feet in the sandals and then gave them back to his brother. "From today on, I shall put on the hermit's dress and live on forest food outside the city walls, awaiting your return," said Bhárata. "I shall place these sandals on the throne under the royal canopy, and they shall rule the kingdom for twice seven years. If you do not return on the last day of the last year, I shall enter the fire and die."

Rama embraced him lovingly and said, "So be it!" Then turning to the people, he said, "Bhárata is pure of heart and a lover of the truth; he will rule you well. When I return from the forest, I shall accept the kingdom from him and with his help, follow the path of my ancestors."

He took leave of them all, bowing low to the priest, his mothers, the ministers, and the citizens and lovingly embracing his two brothers. Bhárata raised the sandals to his head, then placed them on the back of the royal elephant, and the great company returned the way they had come.

When they arrived in Ayodhya, Bhárata did as he had said he would do. He took the queens back to the palaces, then he drove again in his chariot out of the gate of the city, which he would not see again for fourteen years. The ministers and warriors and the elders of the people followed him though he had not spoken to them. He stopped in the village of Nandigrama, not far from the wall, and there he dismounted, and with Shátrughna beside him, spoke to the people.

"My brother, Lord Rama, has given this kingdom to me as a precious trust. Until he returns, these sandals shall represent him. I shall place them upon the throne and raise the royal canopy above them. When Rama returns I shall put them upon his feet again and deliver the kingdom to him."

He lived there in a simple hut and ate a hermit's food;

his wife also put on the hermit's dress and lived there with him, and so did Shátrughna and his wife. All the affairs of state were laid first before the sandals on the royal throne; all gifts were offered there before they were brought to Bhárata and distributed by him. And the people of that kingdom and all the subject kingdoms knew that everything possible had been done to bring Rama back; they saw the faithfulness of his brothers and knew that even Queen Kaikeyi had repented of her wicked deeds. So they took up their occupations again and held their festivals and were happy under the just rule of Bhárata.

7

The Years in the Forest

After Bhárata had gone, Rama decided to leave the lovely mountainside of Chitrakuta and the hut that had sheltered them and to go farther to find another dwelling place. The memory of his brother's anguish and the sorrow of his mother on being again separated from him lingered in that place. Besides, the elephants and horses had broken the young trees and trampled the flowers and grasses and fouled the ground so that the deer and the monkeys did not return there and much of the beauty of the place was gone.

With Lákshmana and Sita he followed the forest paths, for many hermits lived in those woods. They came first to a clearing where a sage lived with his wife, who was as wise and holy as her husband. Indeed, by her discipline and meditation, she had been able during a season of great drought to make the fruits and berries grow abundantly, plump and rich, so that those who lived in the forest might not go hungry.

All of the forest dwellers had heard of Rama's exile and honored him for being so faithful to his father. They honored equally Lákshmana and Sita for following him. So these hermits welcomed the visitors and invited them to stay for as long as they desired. While the two brothers talked with the holy man, Sita sat with his wife, who asked her many things about her marriage and her parents and such things as women like to talk about. Then she went to a chest at the back of her hut and brought out beautiful robes which she gave to Sita. She gave her also ointments and powders. "Use these and your beauty will never fade, nor will these garments ever wear out or lose their colors," she said. "Now dress yourself in them and delight your husband's eyes." And Sita came forth from the hut looking more beautiful than before and showed the gifts to Rama and Lákshmana, who rejoiced with her. They spent the night there and went on farther.

"Let us visit all the hermitages in the forest and talk with these blessed folk," said Rama. "We can learn much from them and spend our years in the forest in their company."

So they went from one to another of the peaceful places where both men and women had come to purify their lives by discipline and meditation and to find God. They could tell when they were nearing a hermitage,

because the animals and birds were tame and did not
flee from them; herds of gentle deer and antelope
browsed in the clearings and birds sang from every tree.
The brothers unstrung their bows as they appoached and
never killed an animal within sight of the holy places.

Everywhere they were made welcome and urged to
stay. A hut was given to them, and the hermits taught
them many useful things: how to find the succulent and
nourishing roots that lay under the ground; which herbs
healed cuts and bruises and which made good medicines;
which wood kindled most quickly into fire when two
sticks were rubbed together. They stayed for long times
in different hermitages, sometimes for two or three
months, sometimes for twelve or more. So ten years of
their exile passed.

In the cold winter evenings or during the summers
when the rains poured ceaselessly from the heavy clouds,
the hermits told them many stories, for most of them
were learned men who had been priests and teachers or
ministers of great kings before they came to the forest.
The two brothers and Sita listened with delight as the
sages told them how the world and all its creatures had
been created, how gods and demons had fought together
long ago. They told how the Lord Vishnu had saved the
world again and again by being born into it in the form
of different creatures.

Once the earth was sinking under the weight of its
population, and Vishnu became a powerful boar who
held it up with his single tusk until it recovered. A
long time ago there was a great flood that washed over

the whole earth, destroying all living things. But there was one holy man called Manu to whom Vishnu appeared in the form of a fish. He told Manu that the flood was coming and bade him build a strong boat with a long rope attached to it and to put into it the seeds of every living plant. So Manu built the boat, and when the waters rose over the earth, the fish returned and towed him and his boat to the one peak in the Himalayas that stood above the flood. There, when the water retreated, Manu recreated the world.

"And once, many thousands of years ago," said the hermit, "a powerful titan defeated all the gods and conquered the three worlds. The gods, with Agni, the lord of fire, leading them, went to Vishnu to beg for his help. This time he was born as a dwarf named Vámana. He grew up in the very hermitage that you protected when you were a boy, O Rama, for he had chosen as his earthly parents two saintly hermits who dwelt in that place. He waited patiently there for the time when he could win back the universe. At last he heard that the titan was about to perform a great sacrifice, and that as part of the ceremony he must give generous alms to all who asked of him. Vámana made himself still meaner by dressing as a begger and appeared before the mighty king.

" 'O lord of the three worlds,' he said, 'will you grant a poor beggar as much land as he can cover with three steps?' The titan laughed as he looked at the little creature and granted the request. Then Vishnu took his own mighty form. He placed one foot on the lower world,

the other on this world that we know, and with the third
step he mounted to heaven. So the universe was saved."

They laughed over this story, and none of them
realized, not even Rama, that the lord Vishnu was dwelling in the world again, in the persons of his brothers and
himself.

As they roamed the woods they went always farther
south, away from Ayodhya. They came to the great
forest of Dándaka, which lies between the Narbada and
the Godávari rivers. In its depths the demons had a
stronghold where Khara, a brother of Rávana, lived with
many followers and whence they went forth, bent on
mischief. In one hermitage many men had gathered
together for fear of these demons. When they saw Rama
and Lákshmana, armed with mighty bows and girded
with swords, they came to them, asking for their help
against the fiends who tormented them.

"O protector of the whole world, you are famed in
earth and heaven for your valor and glory," they said.
"Obedience, justice, and faith are united in you, O Rama.
We beg you to defend and protect the Brahmans and hermits who dwell in this forest and who cannot defend
themselves, since they have foresworn anger and violence.
But you are Kshatrias and have the right to bear and use
weapons, to protect the weak and to slay the evildoer.
Come and behold the bodies of pure-hearted hermits
who have been slain by these demons, while many more
have been carried off and devoured by them! We can no
longer bear their cruel deeds; we have no refuge on

earth but you, O noble princes. Therefore save us from them!"

"I am the servant of the sages," answered Rama. "I have come here out of obedience to my father and, I believe, to deliver you from the demons. Do not fear; my brother and I will slay all those that harm you."

This promise troubled Sita, as if she foresaw the end of their happy life; and one day, as they were resting, she spoke to Rama about it.

"I wish that you were not going into this dangerous forest," she said. "I fear, my lord, that you will be tempted to acts of violence. There are three faults born of desire: one is to tell a lie, the second is to desire another man's wife, and the third is to slay a man without reason. The first two you could never commit, but I fear that if you enter the forest with your great bow in your hand, you may commit the third and slay the demons even if they do not harm you. I beg of you not to do so. You came here to live the life of a hermit. When you return to Ayodhya you can become a warrior again. I say this out of love and respect, O Rama, for how could I dare to teach you your duty? Think about it and do as you think best!"

"Your words are worthy of you, O lovely one, and they please me because one gives advice only to those one loves," Rama replied. "How shall I answer you? I believe that I have come here to protect these blessed ones. I should have had to do so even if they had said nothing; but now they have asked me for help and I promised it to them. How can I break my word?"

When they had visited all the hermitages they entered the Dándaka forest and made a new home for themselves, far south near the Godávari River. They built a strong hut again, of young trees plastered with mud that dried into firm walls; they leveled the floor and thatched the roof with broad, thick leaves. One day they saw a great vulture perched on a nearby tree. They were on the lookout for demons and therefore challenged him, asking him who he was, for they knew that the fiends could take whatever form they chose. The big bird answered them gently, "I am a friend of your father, my children; my name is Jatáyu. My older brother and I are descended directly from those gods who created all the birds and animals in the beginning of the world. I will live near you, if you so desire, O Rama, and I will watch over Sita when you and Lákshmana are away."

In that pleasant place they watched the seasons pass and delighted in the beauty of each one. Sita especially loved their forest life; she was always with Rama now, more than she had been in Ayodhya, where he was often busy with affairs of state and his duty to his father. She had always loved the flowers of her garden and had caged singing birds and taught them to talk to her. Now she had them all around her; they fed from her hand and answered when she called to them. She tamed mynas and parrots and taught them to speak, and when the peacocks spread their tails and danced as the rains began, she could not see enough of them. She loved the deer and made pets of the fawns, which followed her about. It was always a joy to wander in the woods with

Rama, seeking brighter flowers for the garlands she made
for them all, or richer berries and fruit. Rama or Lákshmana hunted, for they never left Sita alone, even
though Jatáyu was there; and the days passed as leaves
fall in the autumn.

Lákshmana served them as he had said he would do
when they set out from Ayodhya. It was he who gathered
the wood and kindled the flame with firesticks; he prepared the meat for cooking, skinned the animals they
killed and tanned the hides for their use. He went far
afield to find the richest berries and the ripest fruit, and
he loved to find the earliest and the brightest flowers for
Sita. When she and Rama returned from walking in the
woods, he brought water and washed their feet. For the
eldest brother was always honored and obeyed by the
younger ones, and when the father died the eldest son
took his place. He protected and cared for his younger
brothers and they behaved to him as sons.

Sometimes in winter and the rainy season they sought
one of the spacious caves in the hills, where they built a
fire at the mouth that kept them warm and dry. "For
nine months the sun has sucked the waters of the ocean
and stored it in these great clouds that rise like mountains
into the sky," said Rama one day as they were kept in by
the rains. "It seems as if we could climb them and crown
the sun with garlands of flowers. Now the lightning
whips them with golden thongs and they groan in pain.
How the cranes love the clouds, circling about them as
if dancing for joy!"

"See how the raindrops fall, like pearls, into the folds

of the leaves!" said Sita. "The birds drink them as if
they were special gifts of the gods. What music we have
here in the forest! The humming of bees, the frogs croak-
ing for joy of the rain, the birds' songs and the thunder
rumbling like the roll of drums seem more beautiful to
me than the instruments of men."

"The rivers are washing away their banks and rushing
toward their lord, the ocean, proud of their speed,"
Lákshmana added. "Our river must be overflowing,
too. Bhárata will have collected the taxes and stored
the grain. He must be celebrating the summer festival."

They rejoiced when the rains stopped, for the autumn
was a lovely season. The clouds that had soaked the earth
and filled the rivers to overflowing were gone, and the
sky was as bright as a drawn sword. The lines of the
mountains were clear and sharp in the sunlight and
loomed dark against the bright stars and in the moon-
light. The rivers ran smoothly and slowly, gradually
uncovering their banks where the wild geese gathered
among the swans and ducks. The elephants that had run
madly through the woods in the spring, seeking and
fighting for their mates, came sedately to the water; they
sprinkled themselves all over through their long trunks
and drank deeply. The peacocks lost their gorgeous tails
and walked forlornly as if ashamed. But the lotus flowers
burst forth in their glory and the forest was filled with
fragrance and with the humming of bees, and the breeze
was cool and sweet. This was the time, Rama and Lákshmana remembered, when kings and warriors set out
for war or conquest.

Winter followed, when the nights were cold and the morning air was biting until the sun, which looked more like the moon than its blazing self, rose high and rejoiced the heart. There were mists in winter: the trees, whose flowers had fallen, seemed asleep, and while the cries of cranes and geese were heard, the birds themselves could not be seen. When the elephants came to drink, they drew their long trunks back again, shocked by the icy stream, and the waterfowl stood on the banks like cowardly warriors who fear the battle. There were clear days, too, and then the three forest dwellers sought the sun and rejoiced in its light and heat.

In the winter evenings, warm and sheltered, they whiled away the time with memories and with stories they had heard in their childhood or from the sages. One time Rama said, "When you told me that you would come with me here, my Sita, you said that you would follow me as Savitri followed her husband Satyavan. Tell us that story now." And Sita, her voice as sweet as any bird's, told them the tale.

Savitri was a proud princess and very beautiful, but when she grew to marriageable age, no man who was worthy of her asked for her hand. One day her father said to her, "It is a shame both to you and to me that you are not yet married. Therefore go forth and seek a husband who is your equal." He gave her a golden chariot and servants to attend her and sent two wise counselors with her to watch over her.

She did not go to the neighboring kingdoms or to fair

cities, but ordered her chariot to go into the forest, where
she visited the holy sages and looked about her. In a
secluded hermitage she came one day upon a blind old
man and his wife who were cared for by their son, a noble
and beautiful youth named Satyavan, the truthful one.
She fell in love with him and he with her. His father had
been a king, but because of his blindness, he had been
driven by an enemy from his throne when Satyavan was
a baby.

Savitri went home and told her father that she had
found a noble husband. He questioned his counselors and
the wise men of his court, and they all agreed that
Satyavan was in every way worthy of his daughter. But
one of them, a seer, said, "There is a single thing against
him which blots out all his virtues. One year after his
wedding day he must die." Nevertheless Savitri would
have no other for her lord; she married Satyavan and
lived with him in the hermitage, caring lovingly for
him and for his parents.

When the year drew to its end, she fasted for three
days and did not sleep; her husband and his parents were
anxious because she was so thin and pale, but she told them
nothing. On the day when she knew he was to die, he
went into the woods with axe in hand to gather fruit and
firewood, and Savitri went with him, though she had
never gone before. In the afternoon he was taken suddenly ill and lay down on the ground with his head on
her lap. Then she was aware of a mighty figure standing
over them, clad in a red robe, a crown on his dark head, a
noose in his hand. She knew him to be Yama, the God

of Death, and she rose and made obeisance to him, after laying Satyavan's head gently down. The god told her that her husband's days had run out, and with that he pulled Satyavan's life out of his body and bound it in his noose. Then he turned away, walking southward.

Savitri followed him, and Yama said to her, "Turn back, O Savitri, and perform the funeral rites of your husband. You are free now of all duty to him and must come no farther."

"Wherever my husband is taken or wherever he goes of his own accord, I go with him," Savitri said. "This is the eternal custom, O lord of death. Besides, it has been said that two people may become friends after taking seven steps together. It is good to be in the company of the righteous, O exalted one."

"I am pleased with your words, O princess," answered Death. "I will grant you a boon—anything except the life of your husband." She asked that her father-in-law might regain his sight. "It shall be so," said Yama. "Now return, O lovely one! Do not weary yourself further."

"How can I be weary in my husband's presence?" asked Savitri. "Wherever you take him, there will I go. You have been called the lord of justice because you deal equally with all creatures, showing no favor. One is never downhearted in the company of the just."

"I have never seen a woman so devoted to her lord," said Yama, "nor heard one speak as you do. Now ask of me a second boon." She asked that her father-in-law might regain his kingdom and always rule it wisely. "He shall regain it soon and never swerve from the path of duty," answered the lord of death. "Now turn back, O gentle lady, for the way is long and you have come far."

"I have not noticed the distance, since I am beside my husband," Savitri replied. "Listen to me further, O chief of the celestials! The righteous are good to others without expecting anything in return; they never injure any creature, but love and protect all beings. Truly, the earth and the sun, the past and the future depend on those who follow the path of virtue."

"The more I listen to you, the more I respect your wisdom and humility, O faithful one," said Yama. "Ask some great boon of me."

"My father-in-law has no sons," she said. "Let sons be born of Satyavan and of me, to carry on his line!"

"You shall have strong and brave sons who will delight your heart," said the god. "Now come no further, for you have already ventured too far."

Then Savitri reminded him that she could not bear Satyavan's sons without her husband. Yama, the just one, saw that he was fairly caught; he undid the noose with good grace, blessing Savitri and all her descendants, and went on his way.

Savitri returned to where her husband's lifeless body lay and took his head upon her lap again. He woke and said, "I have slept a long time. Why did you not waken me, dear one? And where is that dark figure that seemed to stand above me?"

Savitri caressed him lovingly. "I will tell you all tomorrow, O blessed one," she said. "Now let us go home, for the sun set long ago and night has fallen."

"She followed Satyavan not only into the forest, but even to the realm of death," said Sita as she ended the story. "And so I would follow you, O Rama."

"Were Yama's other boons also granted?" asked Rama. "Did Satyavan's father regain his sight?"

"That very afternoon his eyes were opened and he saw his son return from the forest with Savitri," answered Sita. "And a few days later messengers came from his kingdom to tell him that the man who had taken his throne and driven him out had been killed by one of his own ministers. The people wanted their old king back again and did not care whether he was blind or not. So he returned and ruled his kingdom wisely for many years, and when he died, Satyavan became king."

In such wise they spent their time; twelve years and more had now passed by. The demons seemed to be frightened by Rama's very presence and left the forest in peace. Yet the plan of the gods must be carried out, and misfortune came when they least expected it.

8

The Demons Attack

One day Rama, Sita, and Lákshmana were coming back to their hut from the river, where they had been bathing. A female demon, monstrous and ugly, chanced to pass by, and seeing the two youths, so straight and tall and handsome, with Sita, as lovely as the moon, between them, she fell in love with Rama.

"What are you doing in these woods that belong to the demons and why are you in hermit's attire when you are clearly a warrior?" she asked rudely.

Rama told her courteously who they were and asked, in turn, of what race and family she came.

"I am Surpanakha, sister of Rávana, of whom you have no doubt heard. I live with Khara, another brother of mine, not far from here; he rules this forest. O handsomest of men, take me for your wife and we shall wander through the woods and across the summits of the mountains, wherever you please."

Rama smiled and said teasingly, "I am already married and this is my beloved wife; but my brother is without a wife and is young and handsome. Take him for your husband, O lovely one!"

The demon turned to Lákshmana, saying, "Your beauty equals mine, O handsome youth. Let us live happily together in the forest!"

But Lákshmana teased her as Rama had done and answered, "I am but the slave of my elder brother, O large-eyed beauty! Surely you do not wish to be the wife of a servant. He alone is worthy of you."

Surpanakha, furious, turned again to Rama. "It is this ugly, peevish little woman who stands between us. I shall devour her before your eyes, and then we can live happily together." And with blazing eyes she rushed at Sita.

Rama flung her back and said to Lákshmana, "It was foolish of us to taunt such an evil creature. Now she threatens Sita. Teach her a lesson and send her away!" Lákshmana drew his sword, and since he would not kill a woman, cut off her ears and her nose.

Surpanakha gave a terrible shriek and fled howling through the woods. She went to her brother's stronghold, deep in the forest, where he was sitting in his court, and flung herself on the ground, writhing and bleeding.

"Get up!" he said angrily. "Why are you rolling on the ground like a snake? Control yourself and tell us who has dared to disfigure you thus? That fool who has brought you to this sorry plight does not know that he has wound the noose of death about his neck. Tell me, whose body will the vultures tear apart when he has fallen under my blows?"

Surpanakha, sobbing, told him all that had befallen her. "I wish to drink the blood of those two youths and that beautiful damsel," she said.

Her brother called on fourteen powerful warriors and sent them forth, with his sister guiding them, to avenge her. They traveled swiftly, as clouds are driven by the wind, and Surpanakha led them to the hut where the two brothers and Sita were sitting.

"Stay here with Sita, O Lákshmana, while I slay these fiends," said Rama. He stood out in the clearing, stretching his great bow. "We are the sons of the king of Koshala," he said to the warriors. "We live as hermits in these woods and injure no one. Why do you wish to harm us? Halt where you are and come no farther! If you wish to live, turn back, O prowlers of the night!"

"It is you who will die under our blows," they answered, "for you have displeased our master, who has sent us to slay you." And they hurled themselves upon him, letting fly their spears. But Rama, taking fourteen arrows, turned aside the spears, and then with a shout, sped fourteen more, which pierced the bodies of the night-prowlers and entered the earth behind them as serpents enter their holes.

Surpanakha, seeing her avengers slain, sped away, blind with rage, and fell at Khara's feet again, wailing and shrieking. "What is this?" he asked harshly. "I sent fourteen of my best warriors to do your will. Why all these swoonings and wailings?"

She told him that the fourteen had been slain by Rama alone, and Khara was filled with fury. He summoned his whole host, which he himself led. They assembled with a great uproar, the beating of drums, the clash of weapons, and the shouts of those who were eager for battle. Then they went forth like a tempest through and above the forest, like a black storm cloud charged with hail, darkening the sky. Evil omens pursued them: jackals howled, a sign of misfortune in war; birds beat their wings against the demons' banners and their shields. Their leader started to raise a war cry, but his voice died in his throat. Nonetheless he did not turn back, but said with a defiant laugh, "I am able to shoot the stars from the sky and to defeat Indra himself who wields the thunderbolt. Why should I turn back before two men?" And he rushed on toward Rama's hermitage.

The two brothers heard them coming and saw the birds and deer fleeing in terror. "I hear the shouts and drums of our enemies," said Rama. "There will be a great battle and their defeat is certain. See, smoke is rising from my arrows and my bow bends of itself, eager for the string. I see victory already in your face, dear brother. I know that you could strike them down alone, and yet I pray you to take Sita to the cave and guard her there, for we cannot leave her alone during the battle. I can slay these rangers of the night myself." Though he longed to be in the battle, Lákshmana obeyed his elder brother and went with Sita to a well-hidden cave.

Then Rama put on his coat of golden mail; he strung
his bow and twanged its string till the sound re-echoed
from every hillside. He went out to meet that host which
looked like a mass of dark clouds at sunrise, while he
was the sun which would dispel them all. The demons
hurled their spears and arrows at him, and he called
upon the divine weapons given him by the sage when he
was a boy. With one of these he turned aside the demons'
shafts and with another he sent forth not one but a hundred arrows at once that flew like serpents through the
air, each seeking out its foe and piercing his heart. The
demons shrieked and fell, like dry wood consumed by
fire. Again and again he bent his bow like a sickle,
sending forth the deadly arrows that seemed to darken
the sun. He too was wounded, but he stood as calm as a
bull under a downpour of rain. Hundreds of the fiends
were slain and lay upon the field among their fallen
banners, their shields and bright swords, their helmets
and ornaments. The rest fled in terror, but were rallied by
their leader and returned to hurl themselves again upon
Rama, armed with spears, lances, maces, and swords,
while he had only his bow, from which he sent forth the
divine missiles. The fight was so furious that sometimes
it seemed that Rama was winning and sometimes that
his enemies prevailed. Seeing himself surrounded, he
gave a great shout and set upon his bowstring the most
powerful of his weapons, which sent forth a thousand
arrows, each of which found its mark in a demon's
breast.

Then Khara, who had been directing the attack, came

forward in his blazing chariot, for all his host was slain. His horses galloping, he rushed upon Rama as a moth flies to a flame, shooting deadly arrows from his great bow. First Rama cut down his banner, which fell as a flowering tree falls beneath the axe. Then he let fly six well-aimed arrows. Four killed the horses that drew the chariot; the fifth slew the charioteer, and the sixth cut in two Khara's bow at the place where he held it. His bow shattered, his chariot useless, the demon was forced to fight on foot, as Rama did.

He came forward for single combat with a splendid mace in his hand. Rama rested for a moment and said to him, "O dweller in darkness, he who injures others and engages in evil deeds forfeits his life and comes to a miserable end. How can you escape from the fate you invited when you murdered the hermits who dwell in Dándaka? O prowler of the night, however you defend yourself, I shall pluck off your head as I pluck ripe fruit from a palm tree."

"You are a poor creature, O son of a king, for the true warrior does not boast," answered his adversary. "Behold me, with my mace, immovable as a mountain! I shall not only destroy you but the three worlds! Say no more, for sunset is near and our fight must not be stopped by darkness." He hurled his mace, as massive as a thunderbolt, but Rama turned it aside with an arrow and it lay harmless on the earth.

"Is that all that you can do, O disgrace of your family?" cried Rama. "Today the Dándaka forest will be free of you and the blessed ones will live here in peace." He chose an arrow that was made by the gods and shone like fire; it flew, flaming, at Khara's breast and struck it like a thunderbolt. The demon fell, like a forest tree struck by lightning, and gave up his life.

The gods had gathered to watch this conflict; their praises and the music of the nymphs sounded from the sky, while flowers fell upon Rama. Hermits had come from nearby places and others, through their spiritual power, came from afar with the speed of thought; all these gathered round him and praised and blessed him, for now the whole Dándaka forest was free of those evil ones who had lived in it so long. Lákshmana and Sita came forth from the cave and embraced him joyfully; and Sita led him to their hut where she washed and tended his wounds, caressing him with great love.

One demon had escaped the arrows of Rama and sped away from the forest over hundreds of miles of land and ocean, until he came before Rávana himself in his splendid city of Lanka. Surpanakha, too, who had watched the battle and seen her brother and all the host of demons slain, fled to Rávana, who was the head of all their clan. First one and then the other came before him where he sat surrounded by his ministers on the terrace of his palace.

He was splendid to behold, seated on a golden throne in royal garments, adorned with a chain of emeralds, ornaments of gold, and garlands of flowers. His chest was broad and his arms as strong as the trunks of palm trees; they bore the scars of the weapons of the gods which had wounded but could not kill him. Like all of his race, he could assume any form he chose; in his worst shape he had ten heads and twenty arms and was terrifying to behold. He was arrogant in his power and believed himself safe from any enemy.

When he was told that his brother and all his warriors had been slain, he was mad with fury. "Who is this Rama?" he roared. "How does he look? What brought him to Dándaka? Did all the gods come with him to kill my great army?"

"He is a mighty archer, equal to Indra, O great King," answered the demon, still trembling with terror. "He is young and looks like a lion, with shoulders like a bull's; he is as handsome as the full moon. No gods came with him; he destroyed our whole army single-handed with his bow and his flaming arrows that hiss like serpents through the air. Wherever the demons fled in their terror they saw him standing, and so they all were slain."

"I shall go there myself and kill him," cried Rávana. "The gods themselves cannot stand against me; I am the lord of Time, the consumer of Fire, the death of Death itself! I can stop the wind in its course. What can this man do to me?"

"O King, no one in the world, not you and all your kinsmen, can defeat Rama in battle," said the demon humbly. "He is supremely virtuous and brave; he could stop a river in its course and change the boundaries of the sea. He could subdue all creatures if he so desired. Indeed, he could destroy the three worlds and create a new universe. But listen, O ten-headed one, and I will tell you how you can destroy him. Rama is wedded to a

woman more beautiful than any other on earth; indeed,
that slender-waisted damsel is lovelier than any heavenly
being. In some deceitful way, draw Rama and his
brother into the forest, for they never leave her alone.
Then carry her away! Without her, Rama will die!"

Surpanakha, who hated Sita, agreed with this advice.
"No woman in the world has ever been so beautiful. My
ears and nose were cut off because I was trying to bring
her to you, my brother," she said, lying to him.

"It is well," said Rávana. "Tomorrow I will bring that
princess here to my palace."

The following day he mounted his chariot. It flew
through the air, its wheels making a sound like thunder,
and it was drawn by mules with goblins' heads. He
looked down on forests and mountaintops and then on
the shore of the ocean. He crossed it and on the other
side saw a clearing in the forest and a solitary hermitage.
He descended there, for it was the dwelling of his chief
and most trusted follower, Maricha, who was now practicing penance.

Maricha, startled by his coming, bowed to him and
asked, "Is all well in Lanka, O King of demons? Why
have you come hither?"

"Listen to me, Maricha," said his master. "Rama, a
son of Koshala's king, has destroyed my whole army in
the Dándaka forest. He is a worthless fellow; he has
been exiled by his father because of his evil conduct; he
has disgraced the Kshatria caste; he is ruthless and injures others without cause, having cut off the nose and
ears of my sister and destroyed my host. I have resolved

to carry off his beloved wife by force, for that will be my best revenge. Without her, I am told, he cannot live. I want you to help me in this undertaking."

"Whoever advised you to carry off Sita is your deadly enemy, O King," answered his follower. "He might as well have told you to take out the fangs of a poisonous serpent with your bare hands. O lord of Lanka, Sita is dearer to Rama than his own life. Even if you were able to carry her away, he would never rest until he had slain you. You do not know him; you must have very poor spies if they have told you such lies about him. He was not exiled to the forest for any misdeed; he came of his own will, to uphold his father's honor. He is virtue itself; he is self-controlled and gentle and never injures others without cause, but protects all creatures who seek his help. Yet none can stand against his righteous wrath. This great hero is the lord of the whole earth, even as Indra is chief of the gods.

"Listen, O ranger of the night! When he was but a boy I ranged the forest under your orders, sowing terror into the hearts of all creatures. A great sage went to the king of Koshala and asked him to send his son, a boy of fifteen, to drive me and my companions away from his retreat. This was Rama. When I came near the hermitage he struck me with an arrow that flung me a hundred miles into the sea and then he drove all my followers away. Later I met him in the forest, where I was roaming in the form of a deer, with two companions. I despised him because he was in a hermit's dress and I rushed at him with lowered horns. But he, swift as the wind, loosed three deadly arrows from his bow and only by a mighty leap did I escape, while my two companions were slain. Since then, my lord, I see Rama behind every tree; I dream of him at night and wake in terror; if I hear a word beginning with the first two letters of his name, I tremble. For that reason I am here, practicing penance.

"I say this for your own good, O King of demons. Do not rouse that sleeping lion! Do not throw yourself into that inextinguishable fire! No one can defeat Rama in battle. If you take Sita, not only you but the whole city of Lanka, with its temples and palaces, will be destroyed. For who is there to defend it save you, who are the slave of your desires and passions, who know no restraint and listen only to evil counsel? Compare yourself with Rama! O King, there is no greater sin than stealing another man's wife. Return in peace to your own wives and leave Rama with his!"

"O wretch, your words cannot alter my resolve; my mind is fixed," said Rávana angrily. "A wise minister listens respectfully, with joined palms, to what his master says and answers in fitting words. But you forget your duty and speak arrogantly; these gloomy words do not please me. I did not come here to ask for your advice; I came to demand your help, for you are a master of magic. Now listen to my orders! Take the form of a golden deer, flecked with silver, with jeweled horns and hoofs. Show yourself to Sita, for she loves these wild things; play about her so that she will ask Rama to capture you for her. He will pursue you, for he will do anything to please her, leaving Lákshmana with her. Lead him far into the

Rama Aims His Arrow at Khara

forest, and when you are there, imitate his voice and cry out as if in anguish, 'O Lákshmana, save me!' Then his brother will leave Sita and I can easily carry her away. Do this for me and I will give you half my kingdom, O my friend. If you do not obey me, I shall slay you at once. Truly you risk your life by opposing Rama, but certain death awaits you if you oppose me."

Maricha's face wilted with terror; he stared like one already dead at Rávana. Then, licking his dry lips, he answered bitterly, "It is not I who should be pitied for the unexpected misfortune that has come upon me, but you who refuse to hear me, as a dying man refuses medicine. I shall perish as soon as I encounter Rama, and if you succeed, with my help, in bearing Sita away it will be the end of you, of Lanka and of our race. I am doomed, but I had rather die at Rama's hands that at yours. So let us go!"

Rávana embraced Maricha warmly, and they both mounted the chariot. Passing over forests and villages, kingdoms and cities, they came to Dándaka and saw Rama's hermitage, surrounded by palm trees. Nearby, but out of sight, the chariot descended.

9

The Abduction of Sita

Maricha took the form of a little deer, wonderful to behold. Its hide was of gold, dappled with silver, its horns were tipped with jewels that caught the sunlight, and its delicate legs ended in hoofs of emerald. It strayed into the clearing before the hermitage, lifting its delicate head to nibble at leaves, or bending it to taste a flower. It pranced across the grass, sometimes disappearing among the trees, then leaping forth again. It joined the other fawns but they, drawing near with outstretched necks to catch its scent, fled from it in all directions.

Sita was gathering flowers, and her eyes opened wide in wonder and delight as she saw this charming creature. She called to Rama and Lákshmana to come quickly and see it. "O Rama, I have set my heart on this little fawn," she said, laughing with joy. "What grace and beauty! Catch it for me, I pray you, so that I may have it as a pet. We shall take it back to Ayodhya with us and it will delight my mothers, the queens. Even if you cannot catch it, bring me its golden hide, O lion among men!"

"This is a demon who has taken a deer's shape," said Lákshmana. "It is too beautiful to be real. Beware, my brother!"

Rama himself was delighted and wanted to please Sita. "Who would not be charmed by such a fawn?" he said to Lákshmana. "Sita shall have it, alive or dead. If it is a demon, as you believe, I will destroy it. Stay here and guard Sita carefully until I return, O Lákshmana. Do not leave her for a moment."

Rama girded on his sword, took up his bow and his arrows and strode off toward the little fawn. It leaped away into the woods, then lingered until he came close; but as soon as he drew near it bounded lightly away, drawing him ever farther from the hermitage. He saw at last that he could never reach it to capture it: so he fixed an arrow on his bowstring and loosed it at the creature's heart. It leaped into the air as high as a palm tree, then fell to the earth and, as it fell, took Rama's voice and cried out in anguish, "O Lákshmana, save me!" As it spoke, Maricha became himself again and Rama beheld a demon dying at his feet.

"Lákshmana was right," he thought. "I have slain a demon. O, what will Sita do when she hears that cry, 'O Lákshmana, save me!'" A great dread came upon him, and he ran toward the hermitage.

Maricha's cry of distress, in Rama's voice, rang through the forest; Sita and Lákshmana heard it and Sita was terrified. "That is Rama's voice," she said. "Don't you recognize it? He must be in great danger to call out thus. O Lákshmana, go to him at once; he needs you!"

"I dare not leave you alone, Sita," answered Lákshmana. "Rama left you in my care. Do not fear! No god or demon can make him call for help. That cry is a trick. These fiends can imitate other voices and often do so to carry out their wicked plans."

But Sita was frantic with fear and could only think that Rama was in danger of his life. She spoke cruel and unjust words to Lákshmana, her eyes flashing with anger. "Are you your brother's enemy that you do not go at once to help him? Do you want him to die? Have you set your heart on me and wish to marry me when he is dead, or are you the servant of Bhárata? Do you care nothing for his life?"

"Your words pierce my ears like flaming darts, O daughter of Jánaka; I cannot bear them," said Lákshmana. "May all who dwell in the forest bear witness to the bitterness of your answer, when all I desire is to obey my elder brother. I will go, but you may repent this day for having scorned me. May the gods protect you and may you be safe when I return!"

Before he went he drew a circle around the hut with one end of his bow. "Stay within this circle, O Sita, and you will be safe," he said to her. "Do not go beyond it." Then he ran into the forest toward the place whence the cry had come.

Rávana had heard all that had been said and now he came out from among the trees in the guise of a Brahman, dressed in a saffron robe, carrying a begging bowl and leaning on a staff. The breeze stopped and the leaves hung motionless; even the river flowed quietly and no birds sang as he drew near the hermitage. Sita, clad in a yellow sari, her beautiful hair loose on her shoulders, sat weeping on a carpet of leaves before the hut. He stood and looked at her and was smitten by the shafts of the God of Love.

"O lovely damsel, why are you here alone in this forest where terrible demons roam?" he said in a gentle voice. "A sumptuous palace in a pleasant city would suit you better, for I have never seen anyone so beautiful. Are you not afraid to be here? Who are you and to whom do you belong?"

Sita rose and was not afraid, for she had seen many such priests in the forest and he spoke kindly. "Come to the hut, O Brahman," she answered, "and I will give you food, and water to wash your feet."

"I cannot go farther," he said in a feeble voice, "for I am weak from hunger and weariness," and he sank down on the ground. Sita went into the hut and brought a water pot, with fruit and roasted grain laid on a fresh broad leaf. To reach him she had to go outside the circle Lákshmana had drawn, but pity moved her; she hesitated a moment, then stepped across the line and offered the food and water to her guest. All the while she searched the forest with her eyes, longing for the return of Rama.

While the priest refreshed himself, she stood beside him and answered his questions, telling him her story and how Rama had been exiled. "Stay here for a while, O Brahman, for he will return soon from hunting, with fruit and venison. Now tell me your name and family and how you came here."

"I am Rávana, king of the demons, O Sita, before whom gods and men tremble," was the answer. "Beyond the sea, on the summit of a mountain stands my splendid city, Lanka, filled with every delight. O beautiful one, come and live with me there as my chief queen and forget the lot of mortal women. Think no more of Rama who is but human and whose end is near. I, the lord of all the demons, have come to you, pierced by the shafts of love; therefore yield to me, fair princess!"

Sita trembled like a leaf in the wind, but her anger was greater than her fear. "I belong to Rama, who is as steadfast as a rock, as calm as the ocean, who possesses every virtue," she answered. "I belong to him, the greatest of men, and shall ever be faithful to him. O wretch, you can no more win my love than you can grasp the sunlight. You are to Rama as a jackal is to a lion, as iron is to gold, a cat to an elephant, a crow to an eagle! If you should carry me away you would cross the ocean with a stone around your neck, a blazing fire in your robe, for he who insults the wife of Rama, that mighty archer, will never escape death even if he drinks the water of everlasting life!"

"Have you taken leave of your senses?" asked Rávana angrily, striking one fist on the palm of the other hand.

"Have you never heard of my power and valor? I can stand in space and lift the earth; I can pierce the sun with my arrows and drink up the ocean. Behold now, you who let yourself be fooled by any trick, how I can change my shape as I wish!" And he appeared to her in his own form, a splendid demon clad in a red robe and ornaments of gold, looking at her with eyes smoldering with anger.

"If you wish a master famed in the three worlds, yield yourself to me! I am a husband worthy of you," he said. "What binds you to Rama, O foolish one, a man banished from his kingdom at the whim of a woman, who has brought you to a forest full of wild beasts and demons? Leave him and turn to me, for I will do you great honor and never displease you!"

Then Rávana seized her in his powerful arms and bore her to his chariot harnessed to the goblin-headed mules. He mounted, holding her tightly, and the chariot rose into the air. She struggled in vain against him and screamed, "Rama! Rama!" but Rama was far away. Still struggling like a serpent in his grasp, she cried in anguish, "O Lákshmana, do you not see what has befallen me? O Rama, can you not save me?" She looked down in terror at the treetops beneath her and appealed to them. "O flowering trees, tell Rama that I am borne away by Rávana! O beloved river, tell Rama quickly where I have gone! I beseech all creatures that dwell in the forest to tell my lord that his tender love, dearer to him than life, has been stolen away by Rávana."

They had not gone far when she saw Jatáyu, the great

vulture, perched on a branch asleep. "O Jatáyu!" she
called piteously and her voice woke him. "See how I am
being carried off by this wicked demon! Do not try to
stop him, for he is cruel and powerful. But tell Rama
and Lákshmana what has befallen me!"

Jatáyu, though he was old, bore down upon Rávana
on his powerful wings and a terrible fight took place in
the sky. Rávana pierced the great bird with his arrows
but Jatáyu closed in on him, striking him with his sharp
talons and his beak that was like a rock, and wounded
him sorely. Then he attacked the mules and drove them
to earth, where the chariot was broken and the mules
killed. Rávana released Sita and fought the bird on foot,
back and forth, until at last he was able to draw his
sword. He cut off Jatáyu's wings and that ranger of the
skies fell to the earth, mortally wounded. Sita ran to
him, embracing him and weeping over him as if he
were one of her own family. "O fool," Jatáyu said to
Rávana, "you have wound the noose of death round your
own neck."

Then Rávana turned to Sita to seize her again, but she
ran from him, clinging to the trees, screaming for help,
calling upon Rama. But she could not escape him; he
had no chariot, but he caught her in his arms and rose
into the air, for he could travel through it as easily as on
the earth. Her yellow silken robe streamed in the wind
like a sunset cloud; as she struggled in Rávana's grip
the flowers fell from her hair and some of her jewels
broke and fell, flashing, through the air.

She knew that Rama could no longer hear her cries,

but she spoke defiantly to Rávana: "O base wretch, are you not ashamed of what you have done? You did not dare to win me in fair fight, but lured my lord away by magic in the form of a deer. Are you not ashamed to bear away a defenseless woman, the wife of another? You will be forever cursed, O infamous barbarian, for this shameful deed. How do you think you can escape my greathearted lord who alone has destroyed your whole host? You can no more stand against him than a bird can withstand a forest fire. For your own good, set me free at once, O Rávana!"

But Rávana sped on over forests, rivers, mountains, and lakes, carrying his own destruction in his arms. Still looking on all sides for help, Sita saw five great monkeys standing on top of a hill, looking up at the strange sight in the sky. As she passed over them, she took off her jewels, wrapped them in her veil and dropped them, hoping that the monkeys would see them and that in some way they would reach Rama.

Then she saw the ocean beneath her and beyond it a high mountain with a shining city on its summit. Rávana descended there and took her to his palace; he strode into the inner apartments where the women lived. There he set her down and spoke sternly to all the attendants, "Let no one speak harshly to this princess or use her unkindly. Let her have all that she desires of pearls and rubies, robes and ornaments!"

He left her there a while to rest, but soon came back, for he was sorely in love with her and desired to win her. He found her overcome by grief, sitting with bowed head among the demon women, like a doe separated from the herd and beset by hounds. He made her go with him through his palace that was worthy of the gods: through splendid rooms, through courtyards filled with every sort of flower and singing bird; up golden stairways, along galleries upheld by crystal pillars, to windows latticed with gold and jewels, where he showed her the breadth of his kingdom. She saw nothing, for her head was bowed and her eyes downcast and her heart was filled with despair.

"Ten thousand demons, rangers of the night, know me for their lord, O Sita, and each of them has a thousand loyal followers," he said. "My kingdom is surrounded by the ocean and can never be captured, even by the gods. I offer it all to you; rule over it, O lovely one, be happy and live here in eternal delight. Everyone who dwells here and I myself will be your slaves. None can ever take you from my arms. What can you hope from Rama, who has no army and no wealth, not even a chariot? How could he come here even in thought? O Sita, be my queen; my life is yours!"

Sita covered her face with her robe and wept. She plucked a blade of grass and held it between herself and Rávana. "The wise and virtuous king of Koshala had a son who is famed in the three worlds; he is my god and my lord," she said. "It is he and his brother Lákshmana who will rob you of your life. You are like a beast bound to the sacrificial stake; you have but a short time to live. You who cannot be slain by god or demon will not escape alive now that you have brought upon yourself the wrath of Rama. His wife, faithful to her vows, can never be won by a sinner such as you, O last of the demons! Why should a royal swan, playing among the lotuses with her mate, look at a cormorant standing on the bank? Bind or destroy this body of mine; I do not care for my life, but I will never yield to you."

"Think well, O princess!" answered Rávana furiously. "If you do not yield to me in twelve months, my cooks shall cut you to pieces for my morning meal!" For, even among the demons, if a woman was taken unwillingly from her home, she was given a year in which to accustom herself to her new lord and her new surroundings.

Then he called to the attendants of the inner rooms and said to them, "Take this princess to the ashoka grove and guard her well! Sometimes by threats, sometimes by gentle speech, try in every way to break her will as if she were a female elephant." The women took her and pulled her through the palace to the grove of ashoka trees, where the ladies of the court took their pleasure. There, surrounded by those terrible monsters, like an antelope caught in a snare, she gave way to despair and fell fainting to the ground.

10

The Search for Sita

Rama ran back to the hermitage, his heart filled with
dread. Before he reached it, he saw Lákshmana coming
toward him with a pale and troubled face, and his own
fear increased.

"Ah, Lákshmana," he said, taking his brother's hand,
"you have done wrong to leave Sita alone, when demons
are ranging the forest. My heart is heavy. I fear that we
shall not find her and that she has been carried away or
is dead or lost in the woods. Why did you leave her?"

"It was not I who wanted to come hither," said
Lákshmana as they hurried on, "it was Sita who drove
me to it. When she heard your voice cry out, she bade
me go, for she was terrified. I told her that no one in the
three worlds could make you cry out for help, that the

voice must be a demon's, and then she taunted me, saying that I desired your death in order to marry her. That I could not bear, my brother; I was angry and came away to prove her wrong."

"You knew that I could defend myself and yet you abandoned Sita because of a hasty word. Alas, you should not have done so," said Rama. "I tremble to think of what awaits us." And he quickened his pace still further.

When they reached the hermitage they found it empty, the flowers withered, the mats and deerskins scattered here and there; and Sita, who was the heart of it, beautiful and gay and tender, was gone.

"O Lákshmana, where has she gone?" cried Rama, lifting up his arms in a gesture of despair. "Has she been carried away or killed or devoured? Perhaps she has gone to gather fruit or flowers or water from the river. Perhaps she is hiding from us in play."

They searched everywhere, calling her name, through the familiar groves, the caves, along the banks of the river, up the mountain, even though they knew that she never went far from their hermitage alone. Rama came back to the hut exhausted and distracted by grief, and Lákshmana, too, returned from a fruitless search, his mind reeling from grief and terror.

"We have found no trace of her," said Rama. "She must have been borne away by demons, crying out for help from us and we could not hear her. I cannot live without her, Lákshmana; she is dearer to me than my life's breath. How could I return to Ayodhya without her? What could I say to her father, Jánaka, when he

asks for his daughter? Alas, was anyone ever more unhappy than I? Misfortune after misfortune falls upon
me; what evil I must have done in a former life! The
separation from my parents, the loss of the kingdom, and
my exile were all forgotten because we were so happy
living here. But this worst calamity rouses their memory
as fuel revives a dying fire.

"O sun," he cried, leaping to his feet, "you who witness all that takes place on earth, tell me where my beloved has gone, lest I die of grief! O wind, who travels
everywhere, is Sita dead or is she carried off? O trees
whom she loved so well, where can she be found, she
who was as lovely as a young sapling, as radiant as your
blossoms? O beasts of the forests, have you seen her who
tamed the fawns and whose eyes were like a doe's?
Where is she?"

The deer, who loved Sita, came near when he spoke
and turned their heads toward the south, looking upward. Then they moved off, now moving ahead, now
looking back at the two brothers as if to attract their
attention.

"Look at the deer, Rama!" said Lákshmana. "They
are trying to tell us where Sita has gone. Let us go after
them!"

They followed the deer, looking everywhere still for
some trace of the lost one. Rama saw some flowers lying
on the ground. "O Lákshmana," he cried, "I remember
these flowers for I gave them to her this morning and
she put them in her hair. We are on the path that she
took."

They went farther and came upon the place where Jatáyu had fought Rávana, where the earth was trampled and the trees broken. They saw the prints of Sita's feet as she ran hither and thither, and those of Rávana pursuing her, and then a broken bow and the wheel of a chariot. Looking farther they found the broken chariot itself and the dreadful mules lying dead.

"A terrible fight took place here," said Rama. "But to whom did this chariot belong? Whose was this great bow and whose these mighty footprints following those of my delicate love? See, here is a broken necklace—it is hers! O what has happened to her, Lákshmana; where has she been taken?"

Anger blazed up within him; he bound his deerskin garment tight about him and drew his bow, placing a terrible arrow on its string. "If the gods do not bring Sita back to me unharmed, O Lákshmana, I shall blot out the three worlds," he cried, his eyes flashing with wrath. "You will see my arrows fill the sky, stopping the planets in their courses, holding back the wind, darkening the sun and the moon. I shall shatter the crests of the mountains, dry up the lakes and drain the ocean! No being will escape, neither demon, spirit, nor man. If they do not bring back my beloved, I will lay waste the universe and all that is in it!"

Lákshmana had never seen or heard his elder brother in such a mood. "You have always been gentle, controlled and devoted to the welfare of the whole world," he said. "Why must you destroy the universe because of one creature's sin? The fight that took place here was between two warriors; there is no trace of more. The mountains and rivers, the seas and the lakes, the gods themselves are no enemies of yours, O best of men! Now we must find out who has taken Sita away. Let us search everywhere and ask every living creature who he might be. It is he and he alone whom you must destroy. Take courage, O lion among men! Do not yield to despair but remember the wisdom that sorrow has quenched in your heart. If you cannot bear the calamity that has befallen you, how will other men bear theirs?"

Rama came to himself and controlled his anger; he leaned on his great bow and said gently to Lákshmana, "What shall we do? Where shall we go to find her, O my friend?"

There was nothing to do but search farther, so they started again southward. Suddenly they came upon the great body of Jatáyu, the vulture, who was lying mortally wounded.

"O Rama, Sita has been borne away by Rávana, who has taken my life also," said the great bird faintly. "I flew to defend her and threw his chariot to earth and killed the mules. But I am old and my strength failed; he cut off my wings, and leaping into the air, carried Sita away to the south. Do not despair; you will slay him and recover Sita."

Rama knelt beside him, stroking the smooth feathers of his mighty back. "Where has he taken her, O Jatáyu? How does he look and where is his dwelling? O speak further, if you can!" But Jatáyu had given up his life.

Lákshmana gathered wood and built a funeral pyre;

Hánuman Carries the two Princes to Sugriva

they lifted the body of Jatáyu and laid it there and performed the rites as if he had been their father. They went
to the river and offered its water in their cupped hands
to the spirit of the great bird who had died in battle for
their sake and had now gone to the realm of the blessed.
Because of him they knew at last who had taken Sita
away.

Then they went on southward. They were now in the
region that had once been the stronghold of Rávana's
brother, Khara, and his host, whom Rama had destroyed. They met but one demon, a huge and hideous
creature who tried to bar their way. This was a fortunate
encounter. They slew the demon with their arrows, but
as he lay dying he asked them who they were and why
they were there. They told him their names and about
their exile and the loss of Sita.

"Welcome, O tigers among men!" the demon answered. "I have waited a long time for you. Listen to
my story: In former times I was famed for my beauty,
my skill, and courage, but I took on hideous shapes
and amused myself by tormenting the holy ones who
live in the woods. One of them was angered by me and
cursed me, saying that I must always stay in the ugly
form that I had taken. I begged him to take back his
curse, and he had pity on me and said, 'When Rama
burns this body in the lonely forest you will regain your
own shape.' Burn my body now, O noble princes, and I
will tell you who can help you find the princess Sita."

They built the pyre and laid the demon upon it. In its
flames the ugly body was destroyed and from them a

beautiful one arose, clad in spotless raiment and adorned with jewels.

"Listen, O Rama," the demon said. "There is a great monkey named Sugriva who was banished and persecuted by his brother Bali, who is the king of all the apes. These are no common beasts, O lord of men; Bali is the son of Indra and Sugriva is the Sun-God's child. They are powerful and wise and can change their forms at will, even as demons can. Sugriva lives on a lofty mountain near Lake Pampa with a few faithful followers. Since his exile, he wanders restlessly over this whole land; he knows every place and every demon who dwells between here and the southern ocean. Make an alliance with him, O Rama, and he and his companions will find Sita wherever she may be." He told them how to reach Lake Pampa and then leaped joyfully into the sky.

Rama and Lákshmana followed the demon's directions and soon came to Lake Pampa. It was late spring and the water was calm and beautiful, bordered with trees as lofty as hills. Waterfowl swam upon it and deer and elephants came down to drink. But the spring brought no joy to the two brothers, who remembered how Sita had loved that season. They looked for the mountain where Sugriva dwelt.

At the same time that great monkey, Sugriva, was watching them from the mountainside, with four faithful friends who had followed him into exile. He saw that they were warriors, in spite of their hermit's dress, that they carried great bows and were girded with swords. His heart pounded with fear.

"My brother Bali has sent these warriors to kill me," he said to his companions, and they all ran to a higher crest of the mountain, leaping from rock to rock.

When they had reached a safe place, Sugriva's most trusted friend and former minister said to him, "I see no cause for fear, O tiger among the forest folk. Your monkey nature has overcome the god in you. A leader must not give way to fear." The speaker was Hánuman, a son of the Wind-God.

Sugriva was calmed by these words but still doubtful. "Who would not be afraid of two such warriors?" he said. "Go down and speak to them, O child of the wind; find out why they have come here and study them carefully."

Hánuman took the shape of a wandering monk and appeared before the two brothers. "O brave strangers," he said courteously, "you have the air of lions or mighty bulls and seem worthy to rule kingdoms, though you are clad in deerskins. Truly, the sun and the moon have descended on this mountain. Who are you and what brings you to this far and lonely forest?"

"How charmingly he speaks!" said Rama to his brother. "He must know the Vedas and has surely studied grammar, for his speech is correct and he expresses himself very gracefully. Answer his questions freely, O Lákshmana; we can trust him." Lákshmana told him their story and that they were looking for Sugriva, to ask his help in finding Sita.

"It is he who has sent me to you, O mighty warriors," answered Hánuman. "He, too, is exiled from his home by his brother Bali who has kept his wife and driven him cruelly away. He will be your friend, and I, too, will help you in your search. I am Hánuman, the son of Vayu, the bearer of fragrance. I am a monkey, though you see me in a human shape. Come, let us go to Sugriva." Hánuman was pleased, for he thought to himself, "These heroes will restore Sugriva to his rightful place."

He laid aside his disguise and became a mighty ape. He took Rama and Lákshmana, one on each shoulder, and leaped with tremendous bounds up the mountain side to where Sugriva stood. He presented the two princes and told their story. "These great warriors desire your friendship; receive them with honor!" he said.

"It is great good fortune for me, O lion among men, that you desire my friendship, since I am but a monkey," said Sugriva to Rama. "Here is my hand; take it and let us bind ourselves fast with a vow."

Rama took his hand and embraced him warmly, for he believed that these forest folk could help him. Hánuman lit a fire; they worshiped it and walked around it three times, thus making fast their alliance. Then Sugriva broke off a branch of a tree, thick with leaves and blossoms, and offered it to Rama as a seat, while Hánuman did the same for Lákshmana; and they talked together, their hearts filled with hope.

Sugriva told Rama the story of his quarrel with his elder brother Bali. They had gone together to fight a powerful enemy; they had been separated in the fight and Sugriva believed that his brother was dead. He made his way back alone to Kishkindha, the monkeys' capital city, and told the ministers of the kingdom that Bali must have been killed; whereupon they put him upon the throne. But, after more than a year, Bali reappeared and was furious when he found that his kingdom had been taken by his brother, who, he believed, had betrayed him. Sugriva offered him the throne at once and asked his forgiveness, but Bali never relented and drove him out with these few friends and pursued him until at last Sugriva found this refuge where Bali could not reach him.

"I live here in terror, O Rama, for Bali is my enemy, stronger than I," said Sugriva. "I can never return to Kishkindha or see my wife again while he lives. I cannot rest until he dies. O fearless one, free me from this fear!"

"Of what value is friendship if friends do not help one another?" asked Rama. "I shall slay Bali with these arrows that never miss their aim, and you shall regain the kingdom and your wife. I have always kept my word and what I say now shall come to pass, O lion among monkeys!"

Sugriva was overjoyed, and then spoke of Rama's need. "Hánuman has told me why you have come here, O conqueror of foes," he said. "You, too, shall be freed of your sorrow. Whether she is to be found in heaven or hell, I shall bring your beloved princess back to you. I, too, speak the truth and this shall come to pass. Now let me tell you what I have seen with my own eyes. These four companions and I were standing one day on the summit of this mountain when we saw a dark figure like a thundercloud, coursing through the sky and holding in his arms a damsel as beautiful as the dawn. She was struggling in his grasp and cried out, 'O Rama, O Lákshmana!' I did not know then who she could be, but now I know that it was Sita. She saw us and wound her jewels in her veil and threw them down to us. I will bring them to you and you will recognize them."

"O go quickly, my friend, and bring them!" cried Rama.

Sugriva went to a deep cave and brought them forth and laid them in the hands of Rama, who wept as he beheld them, for he knew each jewel and the golden veil. "O Lákshmana," he said, "look upon these bracelets and these earrings, this anklet that Sita threw down in her flight!"

"The anklet is indeed hers, for I have often seen it when I greeted her," answered his brother. "The others I could not recognize, for I never looked above her feet."

"Where does Rávana live, O king of the forest folk?" asked Rama. "Where can I find him that I may slay him?"

"I do not know where he lives," answered Sugriva, weeping for his friend's sorrow. "But do not despair; we shall find him and slay him and all his followers. Banish your sorrow and rouse your courage, O Indra among men! We shall both be victorious!"

The next morning Rama said to Sugriva, "Today you shall see Bali fall like a cleft mountain, struck by these arrows winged with heron's feathers. Let us go at once to Kishkindha."

But Sugriva was still terrified by his brother's power. "I am sure that you can burn up the world with your arrows, yet I still do not know who is stronger, you or Bali," he said. "He can break off the tops of mountain peaks, toss them into the air and catch them again; he can snap in two the tallest forest trees. Before sunrise he can stride from the eastern to the western ocean. If you can pierce one of these great trees with your arrow, O lion among men, I shall believe that you can overcome him, for his breast is like a rock."

Rama smiled and took up his bow, fitting a powerful arrow to its string. Drawing the bowstring to his ear, he loosed his arrow, which pierced seven great trees and returned to his hand. Sugriva was delighted.

Then they started for Kishkindha, and after a long journey over mountains and rivers, they reached the handsome city, built in the hollow of a mountainside. Rama and Lákshmana stayed nearby in the woods while Sugriva went forward to the gate and challenged his brother with a defiant roar. Bali rushed forth in a fury, and a terrible fight took place as the brothers struck each other with their fists as hard as rocks, and bit and tore one another. They were so closely intertwined and their tawny bodies were so much alike that Rama did not dare to shoot his arrow. Sugriva was beaten and ran back to the forest, exhausted and covered with blood.

"Why did you not help me, O Rama, as you promised to do?" he asked reproachfully.

"You were so much alike that I feared to kill you both, dear friend, or to kill you instead of your brother," answered Rama. "O Lákshmana, pluck a strand of that blossoming creeper and wind it round Sugriva's neck, so that I can tell him from Bali. Now have no fear, O hero, for Bali shall die today."

Sugriva, with renewed courage and the bright garland around his neck, went again to the gate and roared out his challenge. Again Bali came forth, panting with rage, and hurled himself at his brother. Though Sugriva fought fiercely, he was the weaker of the two, and soon he made a sign to Rama, who stood behind the trees, an arrow on his bowstring. He loosed it and that terrible arrow, shining like flame, pierced the breast of the king of monkeys who fell like a mighty tree cut by the axe or like a banner overthrown on the battlefield.

Rama and Lákshmana came to him slowly and looked with respect at that great king, his long arms lying powerless, his broad chest adorned with a golden chain, wrought with a hundred lotuses, given to him by Indra. "How could you strike me from behind, while I was fighting with another, O prince?" asked Bali proudly. "I have always heard that Rama is noble, generous and brave, dutiful, and devoted to the welfare of all creatures. I have not harmed you in any way; I am a monkey living in the woods on fruits and roots. But you are the son of a king and you wear a hermit's dress; how can one who belongs to the Kshatria caste and wears the garb of holiness do such a wicked thing? How will you answer for this deed to those who follow the path of virtue?"

"Why do you reproach me, O Bali?" asked Rama. "You yourself have broken the laws of virtue and have met with just punishment. A younger brother should be cherished as a son, but you have mercilessly driven out Sugriva and made his wife your own. A brother's wife should be looked upon as a sister, and marriage with a sister is punished by death. The virtuous Bhárata rules the whole earth, and we, his brothers, obey him and punish those who overstep the limits of the law. Sugriva is my friend and I have promised to end his exile and restore his wife to him. Judge for yourself if your punishment is right, O brave lion among monkeys."

Bali was silent and his breath was nearly gone. His eyes fell on Sugriva and he said faintly, "It seems that we were not destined to live at peace with one another, O Sugriva, though it is natural for brothers to do so. Though I have wronged you, I beg you to be a father and a guardian to my young son, Angada, who is brave and worthy of happiness. Now take my golden necklace; you will today be king of the forest, while I am going to the realm of death." Speaking thus, suffering greatly from his wound, his eyes wild and his big teeth chattering, Bali gave up his life.

There was a great uproar and lamentation from the monkeys, for Bali had been a good and powerful king and they felt very safe under his rule. They performed his funeral rites with great splendor, and even Sugriva wept over him, saying to Rama, "The first time I fought against my brother, he could easily have killed me, but he only said, 'Begone, and never come here again!' whereas I have brought about his death. I have done a vile and ignoble thing."

However, as soon as Bali's great body had been burned
by the bank of the river and all the rites were over, the
coronation of Sugriva was to take place, and the grief of
the monkeys was quickly changed to joy and festivity.
Hánuman asked Rama to take the place of honor at the
ceremony. "Sugriva will pay homage to you and give
you garlands and jewels and precious perfumes, O lord
of men," he said. "Come and behold our city, which is
carved out of the mountain, and live in splendor there!"

"I have taken a vow, O Hánuman, and may not enter
a city or even a village for fourteen years, thirteen of
which have now gone by," said Rama. "Lákshmana and
I will live here on the mountain in this spacious cave
until the rainy season is past. The rains will soon begin,
and no army can move, no traveler set forth, till they
are over and the earth is dry again. When autumn comes
we shall start upon our search. Meanwhile return to
Kishkindha, dear friend, and see Sugriva crowned."

The monkeys poured back into their city, leaping and
frolicking, and Sugriva was duly installed as their king,
with Bali's son, Angada, as crown prince. There was
great festivity in the city, whose streets were filled with
a merry crowd carrying flags and banners and beating
drums and cymbals.

These were the monkeys who had been born of the
gods and the nymphs at the behest of Brahma the creator, to help Rama carry out the plan that had been
made in heaven. Their tawny bodies were clothed as
men's are; they adorned themselves with gold and
jewels; they lived in fine houses and made music and

held high festivals. They could change their size, becoming as small as cats or as large as clouds, if the need arose, and could take other shapes, as Hánuman had done when he met Rama, and as the demons could. Clubs and stones and their own fists and teeth were their only weapons, but they were powerful fighters, well able to defend their own people or to help a friend.

Yet they were monkeys still, fickle, and quick to change from joy to grief, from boastfulness to terror, and they easily forgot where they were going if they saw a tree full of ripe fruit. They and Rama had met at last and were soon to begin the task that destiny had set for them.

11

The Monkeys' Search

The months of the rainy season seemed like a year to Rama and Lákshmana, who were unable to move while the clouds poured out their load of life-giving water. They did not know whether Sita was alive or dead or what terrible things might be happening to her while they could do nothing to save her. Rama might have despaired if it had not been for the quiet courage and devotion of his brother. They both trusted Sugriva to start the search for Sita as soon as the rains were over and it was possible to do so.

Autumn came at last; the sky cleared and the sun and the moon shone brightly. The rivers, which had over-flowed the banks, ran quietly again, and the waterbirds gathered on their sandy beaches. The grass, the flowers,

and the blossoming trees were fresh and beautiful after
the rain and the earth slowly dried.

But there was no move from Sugriva. That great
ranger of the woods, restored to the delights of his kingdom after a long exile, was enjoying himself thoroughly.
He had regained his wife, whom he loved dearly, and
had also made Bali's widow, who was very beautiful, one
of his queens. Charming monkey maidens waited upon
him, and he spent his time roistering and drinking too
much of the wine that the forest folk made from honey.
Hánuman, who was wiser than Sugriva, spoke to him of
his duty to Rama, but still nothing happened.

After many days had passed, Rama said to Lákshmana, "The time when kings declare war on one another
has come, but I do not see that Sugriva is preparing to
go forth. He promised that at this time we should set
out, but he has forgotten his pledge. Go to Kishkindha,
O my friend, and say to Sugriva in my name, 'Honor the
promise you made to me, O King of apes, or you may follow the path taken by your brother! The gate of death,
through which he passed, is not closed, O Sugriva!' "

Lákshmana, filled with anger, went for the first time
to that splendid city of Kishkindha, hollowed out of the
mountain. The monkeys who guarded the gates saw
his wrath and dared not question him but stood with
joined palms as he passed. He strode through the streets,
past houses and gardens, meeting handsome monkeys
wearing garlands and fine raiment. They fled in fear before his angry glances, and two of them ran to the palace
and told Sugriva that Lákshmana was coming, but their

king was in a drunken slumber and did not hear them.
Lákshmana entered the palace without hindrance, and
as he went through the courtyard he heard music and
the tinkling of anklets. This infuriated him anew as he
thought of his brother waiting in the cave, and he
stretched the cord of his bow and twanged it. The sound
echoed through the palace like a clap of thunder, and
Sugriva, hearing it, came to himself and trembled. He
rose as Lákshmana entered and stood before him with
joined palms, his wives following like a cluster of stars
around the moon.

"You are an ignoble, false, and ungrateful wretch, O
monkey," said Lákshmana. "Rama has given you all
that you asked and you do nothing in return. This is
his message to you: 'The gate of death is not closed, O
Sugriva; honor your promise, lest you follow Bali!'"

Sugriva answered him humbly, and then said to
Hánuman, who stood near, "Send forth messengers at
once and call together all those who dwell on the farthest
mountains and the farthest shores of the sea; those who
live in the caves and in the vast, fair and fragrant forests!
Summon them from every quarter of the earth with all
speed and command them to be here in ten days' time!"

Hánuman obeyed him gladly, and the messengers
went forth at once in all directions. Then Sugriva and a
great crowd of his followers went with Lákshmana to the
cave where Rama dwelt, and when he saw him, fell at
that hero's feet, touching them with his forehead. And
when Rama heard what had been done he was pleased;
his face cleared and was as bright as a lotus blossom.

Before the ten days were over, a cloud of dust rose over the forest and the trees trembled as if a tempest were coming. Monkeys poured down all the mountainsides, leaping and gamboling and shouting. Some were as black as panthers; those who frolicked on the western hills shone like gold; those from the northern mountains were as tawny as a lion's mane, and others were as white as the moon. They came from all over the earth at Sugriva's command, from mountain, river, forest, and seashore, till the woods and hillsides around Kishkindha could hardly hold them.

When they had assembled, their leaders came to their king, where he stood beside Rama and Lákshmana. They bowed before him and offered him gifts of fruits and flowers and healing herbs.

"Here are all the monkeys in my kingdom, O Rama," said Sugriva. "They are wise and brave, untiring, and famous for their noble deeds. They have come to serve you; it is for you to order them as you see fit."

"It is not for me or for Lákshmana to command this expedition, O lord of the forest," answered Rama. "You must lead it. You know my purpose: first we must find out where Rávana dwells and whether Sita still lives; then we must rescue her and slay the wretch who stole her away."

Sugriva divided his forces into four groups, giving each one a mighty leader. He sent one group in each direction, east, west, north, and south and said to their leaders, "Search carefully in every place that can be searched by climbing, running, or swimming, for the daughter of Jánaka, the beloved wife of Rama, and for the king of all the demons, Rávana, who carried her away. Explore the forests, rivers, caverns, the mountain-tops, the shores of the seas and the islands. Go to the very ends of the earth but not beyond its awful limits, or you will never return. He who shall come back within a month, having found Sita, will spend his days in happiness, sharing all I possess. Return within the month whether you are successful or not; he who is late will be put to death."

Sugriva gave Angada, the son of Bali, the command of the expedition to the south, where Sita was most likely to be found, since she had last been seen carried by Rávana in that direction. Since Angada was young and inexperienced, he sent Hánuman with him, for he trusted Hánuman above all his other counselors. "I do not know of anything in the earth, in the sea or the sky that can hinder your course, O mighty one," he said. "You have speed, skill and energy, strength, wit and courage. Use them all to find Sita, O best of monkeys!"

Rama heard these words and thought to himself, "This lord of the forest has great faith in Hánuman, whose deeds must have deserved his master's trust. He will probably be the one to succeed in his quest." A wave of hope flooded his heart, and he gave Hánuman the only ornament that he had kept, a ring inscribed with his name.

"Show this to Sita, O foremost of monkeys, and she will know you to be my messenger," he said. "I depend on your valor and believe that you will succeed. O Hánu-

man, O son of the wind, do all that is within your power
to find the daughter of Jánaka!"

All the monkeys set out, as they had come, with a
great uproar, in clouds of dust, like four swarms of
locusts. "I shall defeat Rávana in single combat, and I
shall say to Sita, 'Rest now, O princess, you are weary!'"
said one. "I shall find her, if I have to cleave the mountains or penetrate the earth or the ocean." "I can jump
four miles in one leap," said another. "I can clear a
hundred," said a third. "Nothing can stop me," another
boasted. "We shall surely slay Rávana and bring Sita
back."

The expedition led by Angada traveled southward
speedily, for the monkeys were excited and full of hope.
During the days they went forth in every direction,
searching the mountaintops, the caverns, the forests, the
ravines; at night they met at an appointed place and re-
ported what they had seen. Nowhere did they find a
trace of Rávana or of Sita. Each night they lay down to
sleep, tired out and disappointed; each morning they
rose with new hope and courage.

They came at last, far to the south, to a solitary region
where nothing seemed to grow, where the streams had
dried up and there were no pleasant pools covered with
lilies. Animals and birds had left it, and they found
neither fruit nor roots, on which they lived. Hungry,
thirsty, thin and woebegone, they sat down under the
trees. While they rested, they noticed what looked like
the mouth of a cave, though it was overgrown with
bushes and creepers. Out of it flew swans and geese and

other fowl, and drops of water fell from their breasts
and wings, which were dusted, too, with the pollen of
lotuses. The monkeys were amazed and went nearer to
the opening, a little frightened, but so hungry and thirsty
that they went in, holding each other's hands, as they
explored the dark entrance. Soon they saw a light ahead
of them, and they came out into a lovely place filled
with fruit trees, running streams and pools of water.
Honeycombs hung from the trees and there were flowers
everywhere. Though it was underground, it shone with
its own light; golden trees encircled it, that gleamed like
the first light of dawn, with blossoms as bright as jewels;
in the pools golden fishes and turtles swam, and blue
lotuses bloomed on the quiet waters. Then the monkeys
saw that palaces were built among the trees, adorned
with gold, silver, and many-colored gems and little latticed windows hung with pearls; yet no one seemed to
live there.

As they wandered in amazement about this wonderful
place, they came upon a woman seated under a tree, clad
in hermit's garments and thin with fasting. Hánuman
bowed down to her, with joined palms, and told her
who they were and how they had come there. "To
whom does this retreat belong?" he asked her. "Who
has produced these golden trees, these pools and palaces?
We are so amazed at all these marvels that we have
nearly taken leave of our senses."

"This golden grove was built by Maya, the chief architect of the demons, O foremost of monkeys," she answered. "He practiced severe discipline in the forest for

many years and was granted by the gods the mastery of his art. He built this for a nymph whom he loved dearly; she is skilled in dancing and singing and entertains the gods in their celestial halls. She is my dear friend and I guard this place for her. Take what you will; rest and refresh yourselves."

In that magic garden the monkeys lost all sense of time and lingered there until the month Sugriva gave them for their search had run its course. Then Hánuman went to her who guarded it and told her that they must go and asked her how they could depart, for they had all forgotten where the entrance was. "It is hard for any living being to leave this cave," she said, "but through my spiritual power I will deliver you. Now close your eyes, for none may leave here who can see." All the monkeys covered their eyes with their slender fingers, and in a moment they were outside the cave, standing on a mountainside and looking down upon the vast ocean, which had no limit as far as their eyes could see.

They sat down and looked at it with awe, and their hearts sank. "What are we to do now?" Angada asked. "We are far from home and our time has run out. We have no news of Sita. If we arrive late, having failed in our quest, Sugriva will never forgive us. Let us stay here and die of hunger, rather than return and be put to death." Most of the other monkeys, in despair, agreed with him, but one great warrior said, "Why should we give up and die? Let us return to the beautiful place we have just left and live there forever. There we need fear no one, for we found the entrance only by chance."

All the monkeys except Hánuman and one or two of the wiser ones agreed with him happily. "You know very well, O conqueror of your enemies, that we monkeys are fickle by nature," said Hánuman. "If we return to those pleasant groves, we shall very soon miss our wives and sons and wish to go home. The entrance to that land, which you think so safe, cannot escape the eyes of Rama and Lákshmana. I believe that if we return, humbly asking for forgiveness, Sugriva will grant it."

"Who could trust that treacherous and wicked one, who caused the death of his elder brother and forgot his debt to Rama?" answered Angada. "All he cares about is to keep his power and his kingdom, and he would gladly be rid of me, who am the son of Bali and his rightful heir. I shall never return to Kishkindha. It is better to die here than to meet a cruel death at home." He spread some grass on the hillside and sat down, facing the sea, and all those high-souled monkeys gathered grass and sat down, weeping, and resolved to starve to death. The whole mountainside resounded with lamentations.

Now it happened that a great vulture was sitting on the top of the mountain above them. He was the brother of Jatáyu, who had tried to save Sita; he was an old and noble bird and he could not fly because his wings had been burned. So he ate what he could reach from where he sat, and his son brought him food now and then. He heard the monkeys' decision and said happily, "Every man reaps the fruit of his former deeds. The good that I have done has brought me these monkeys; I shall eat them one by one as they die."

Angada saw him and was reminded of Jatáyu, whose story he had heard from Rama. "Behold, death has come to us in the form of this vulture," he said to Hánuman. "Jatáyu willingly gave his life for Rama, and we, too, are about to die because we came here to serve him. Happy is Jatáyu, for he is now free of all fear and dwells in the realm of the blessed."

The vulture heard this and cried out, "Who speaks of the death of my brother, dear to me as my life? It is a long time since I have heard his name; how did he come to die? I cannot fly, O people of the forest, because my wings were burned long ago when I was young. Pray help me to come down to you and tell me more."

A few of the monkeys leaped up the mountain and helped the great bird down; then they told him the whole story of Rama and the carrying away of Sita and the brave death of his brother Jatáyu.

"It is because of my brother that my wings were burned, O rangers of the woods," said the vulture. "When we were young we were proud of our power and tried to reach the sun. We flung ourselves on the currents of air and rose higher and higher, till the mountains looked like rocks and the rivers like threads binding the earth together. As noon came near, Jatáyu weakened and I covered him with my wings to shield him from the fierce rays of the sun. He flew off in safety, but my wings were scorched, and I fell here upon this mountain and have never heard about him since that time. Nonetheless, though I cannot fly I can still serve Rama. Last spring I saw Rávana flying through the air and in his arms was a young and beautiful woman who cried out, 'O Rama! O Lákshmana!' Without doubt she was Sita.

"Now listen, O most excellent monkeys, and do not despair. Rávana lives in Lanka, a city built by the gods, which lies a full hundred miles from here on an island in the ocean. Show your valor, O conquerors of foes; find some way to cross those miles of water and find Sita. Then return with your purpose fulfilled. Rávana cannot stand against the arrows of Rama and Lákshmana. He will be slain, and I shall be avenged for my brother's death. Surely I fell upon this mountain in order to help you in this search, for behold, my wings are growing again and I feel as strong as I did in my youth."

He told them the nearest point on the shore to Lanka, and then flew joyfully up to the mountaintop. The monkeys were filled with delight; they felt as strong as lions and jumped about, shouting with joy. They leaped and ran down to the place the vulture had told them about, but were sobered again when they beheld the limitless ocean with no island anywhere in sight. "What shall we do now?" they cried. Their leaders met together and the rest of the monkeys sat around them, awaiting their decision.

"Which of us is able to leap a hundred miles across the ocean?" asked Angada. "Who can carry out the command of the king and free us of our fears? What brave monkey can enable us to return to our wives and children, crowned with success, and to face Rama and Sugriva with light hearts?" No one spoke a word, and the whole company seemed to be stunned by this question. "Tell us," repeated Angada, "how far each of you is able to leap over the sea?"

"I can leap a hundred miles," said one. "I can leap two hundred," cried another. "I can easily leap a hundred," said a third, "but could I return? That is the question."

The eldest of the monkeys, old and wise, said, "Alas, I no longer have the strength for such a deed, but I know one who can leap over and back without difficulty." He called upon Hánuman who was sitting quietly by himself. "Why are you sitting there silent, O son of the wind? We are lost unless you put forth your power, intelligence, and courage to save us, for you alone can do it.

"When you were still a child, you saw the sun rise red one morning over the forest and you thought it was a fruit and tried to seize it. You bounded high into the air, and with the power you got from your father, you rushed upward toward the sun with outstretched hands. Then Indra, the lord of heaven, saw you intruding into his realm and hurled his thunderbolt against you; you fell upon a mountain and broke your jaw against a rock. Therefore you are called Hánuman, the one with the broken jaw. Your father picked you up and carried you to a cave, where he held you on his lap till you recovered consciousness. He was so angry that he stayed there with you, depriving all the rest of the universe of his presence, and there was great suffering in the world, for he gives breath to every living thing. All life and movement ceased, and the gods were alarmed. They gathered about the cave, and bestowed many boons upon you in order to make peace with your father—Vayu, the life-giver, the bearer of fragrance. Each one promised that his power and his weapons would never be used against you; that you would never be wounded in battle; and that god of a thousand eyes who had loosed his thunderbolt against you promised that you should never die until you desired to do so. These boons will bring you safely back to us.

"Now bestir yourself, O lion among monkeys, and cross the vast ocean even as Vishnu crossed the whole universe with his three strides!"

Hánuman rose in the midst of them, and all the monkeys began to shout and to praise him. He waved his tail, and his hair rose on end as he felt his power flow into him; he was like a lion stretching himself at the mouth of his cave. "I am the son of him who shatters mountains and is the friend of fire, whose kingdom is space. I can leap beyond the stars and planets and cause the ocean to overflow, or I can dry it up," he cried. "In a moment I shall fly through the air as lightning leaps from a cloud and reach Lanka in the wink of an eye. My heart tells me that I shall find Sita; therefore rejoice! When I have turned Lanka upside down I shall come back to you."

"O hero, O elephant among monkeys!" cried the others. "We shall stand on one foot, awaiting your return."

12
Hanuman's Leap

Hánuman climbed to the top of the nearest mountain and the others followed him and stood watching as he chose the best place to start his leap. He began to increase his size until he was as large as a cloud. He paid homage to the gods and turned to the east to salute his father, Vayu. Then he stiffened his arms and legs and crouched down, summoning all his strength and courage. Under the pressure of his limbs the mountain trembled; water gushed forth from its cracks, gold and silver veins split open and glittered in the sun, and the trees tossed and scattered their blossoms on all sides. Looking ahead toward his goal, he drew in his breath, pressed his feet firmly down, flattened his ears, curled his tail up over his back, and sprang into the air, his two arms outstretched before him. He was like a meteor rushing through the sky and his shadow cast on the waves looked like a mighty ship.

Hánuman sped on over the ocean, following the path of the birds. He scattered the clouds before him, sometimes entering them, then hidden by them, then emerging again, as the moon does. All the elements helped and blessed him, for they knew his errand: the sun did not scorch him, the winds favored him, and the water was calm. The gods and their attendant nymphs were watching him; they sang his praises and let fall celestial blossoms on his path.

Not all creatures were favorable to him. As he neared the shore of Lanka, a female demon of enormous size saw him sailing through the air and wished to devour him. She seized his shadow and he felt himself held fast, like a ship becalmed at sea. He looked down and saw her vast, wide-open mouth. "You are destined to be my food, O foremost of monkeys; therefore enter my mouth, for I am about to devour you," she said.

"I have been sent to find Sita, the beloved wife of Rama," answered Hánuman. "When I have found her and told Rama where she is, I will return and enter your mouth; I promise you in good faith."

"None may pass me alive," she said. "Enter my mouth and then go your way, if you can." She opened her mouth still wider and put herself in Hánuman's way.

He was angered by her persistence. "Then open your mouth wide enough to swallow me," he said. She opened it wider and he increased his size, and the wider she opened it the huger he became, hovering over her like a great cloud. Finally, when her jaws were about a mile apart, he changed into a tiny monkey and dashed into her mouth and out again. "I salute you!" he cried, growing big again and speeding on his way. "I have entered your mouth; now I go to seek Sita!"

After that nothing stood in his way. He soon beheld a wooded shore and landed there unseen by anyone. Though he had just crossed the unconquerable sea without pausing for breath, he did not feel at all tired.

"If any demon has seen me in the air and then meets me in this gigantic form, he will suspect and question me," he thought, and took his own shape again, a monkey whom no one would notice. He leaped up on a hill and from there he saw the noble city of Lanka perched on the summit of a mountain, its golden walls gleaming in the sun, its turrets decorated with gay flags and pennants. He passed through woods fragrant with honey and blossoms, through green fields, past ponds and rivers, and came to the city. Its golden walls rose high before him and behind them its palaces appeared like autumn clouds. He looked at it with awe, for it was like a city of the gods, and so it was, for the architect of the gods had built it long ago for Rávana's elder brother. He came to the northern gate, flanked with splendid towers, and saw that it was closely guarded by warriors with dreadful weapons. Hánuman's heart sank.

"Even if Rama could reach this place, what could he do?" he thought, sighing deeply. "There are only three among us who are powerful enough to cross the ocean—

Angada, Sugriva and I. But let me first find Sita. I must be very careful, for everything depends on me. If I am caught, all will be lost. I think that I had better wait for the night and make myself very small in order not to be noticed."

So he sat in a tree, eating its fruit, until the sun set. When dusk came, he grew smaller until he was about as large as a cat, and sprang up onto the wall of Lanka. He saw wide streets and fine houses with balconies and archways resting on golden pillars. Each had its garden filled with flowers, and there were groves of trees and pools of clear water in the city's squares. He heard voices and laughter, the sounds of drums and cymbals, the clapping of hands, and the tinkle of women's girdles and anklets. Running along the roofs, leaping from one to another, he looked into the courtyards and the rooms, lit with lamps and torches, and noted the richness and beauty of those mansions, fragrant with flowers and incense. As he went from one to another the moon rose and filled the world with its light. It was at the full and shone like a seashell, like a lotus blossom or a swan resting on a lake; it rose into the sky as a lion comes forth from its cave, as a lord of elephants enters the forest, or as a king sets forth to view his dominion.

Hánuman could see everything now as clearly as if it were day. He came at last to a great palace which he knew must be Rávana's, for it was encircled by a wall decorated with royal symbols and guarded by fierce, armed demons. The wall surrounded a vast domain: the rooms and courts of the palace seemed endless, and be-

yond them were storehouses, armories, and stables for
great elephants and war horses; besides the lovely gardens, there were groves of trees chosen for their blossoms
and fragrance, where rare deer and birds of every kind
abounded. It was in this palace that he would find Sita
if she were still alive.

No one noticed the slender little monkey who might
have wandered in from any garden, and Hánuman went
boldly into the heart of the palace, where he beheld a
vast and glorious hall. Its roof was held up by delicate
columns of crystal and gold, its floor was inlaid with
coral and ivory, partly covered with a wide carpet that
showed all the kingdoms of the earth and its rivers and
seas. Light stairways led to galleries and rooms above,
lost in the haze of incense. The hall was lighted by lamps
upheld by the branches of golden trees or hanging by
jeweled chains from the galleries. "Is this paradise, or
the city of Indra, the lord of heaven?" Hánuman asked
himself.

The great hall was lighted and filled with people, but
it was silent because they were all asleep, for the night
was half spent. It was here that Rávana reveled with his
queens and the lovely damsels, musicians, and dancers
who waited upon him. All of them now lay on the wide
carpet like lotuses and lilies that close their petals at evening. Their wreaths had fallen from their heads, their
hair was unbound, and their silken garments, of every
lovely hue, were in disarray. The limbs of the dancers
were as beautiful in sleep as they were in the dance; the
musicians still held their instruments in their hands as

if they were beloved companions. One had her arms
about her lute; another pressed her tambourine to her
breast; the fingers of a third, in her sleep, still gently
touched her drum. Rávana's queens slept on rich couches,
and all were tired out with feasting and dancing and
singing.

Then Hánuman shrank back with sudden fear; he ran
up a stairway and stood on a landing, his body pressed
against the wall. For he saw a splendid dais covered with
rich rugs, and on it a couch under a white canopy that
shone like the moon. There lay the king of the demons
himself, Rávana, like a purple thundercloud, while the
light playing on his diadem, his flashing earrings and
jeweled ornaments made them look like lightning issu-
ing from that cloud. His vast arms, scarred by the weapons of the gods, lay relaxed on the beautiful couch like
two angry serpents asleep in a cave; a string of pearls lay
across his mighty chest, and he breathed with a hissing
sound. The damsels who served him lay at the foot of
the couch and on the dais, clad in lovely garments and
adorned with jewels and garlands.

"Sita could never be here," Hánuman thought to himself. "Apart from Rama she could not feast or adorn
herself, nor would she ever yield to another lover." He
left the banqueting hall and explored every room in the
palace, going up and down, to and fro, opening some
doors and closing others, till there was not the space of
four fingers that he had left unseen. He was in despair,
fearing that Sita must be dead and that Rama would
also die if he brought no news of her. Then he came out

from the palace into a beautiful grove of ashoka trees, and hope sprang up in his heart again.

"Here, surely, I shall find her," he thought. "She loved the forest, and she will have come here because it reminds her of her happy years with Rama."

He leaped into the branches and looked about him. All at once he saw a woman sitting under a neighboring tree, awake and weeping. Her yellow robe was faded and dusty, her thick hair was bound in one long braid down her back; she wore no jewels and was thin and weary. Around her, demon women lay asleep, and as she looked about her with eyes wide with fear, she was like a gazelle surrounded by a pack of hounds.

Hánuman sat in the tree, wondering if this were truly Sita and if so how he could speak to her without frightening her. While he sat there the sky lightened and dawn came; within the palace he heard music and the chanting of the Vedas. Then he saw Rávana striding into the grove in gorgeous raiment, followed by a crowd of women, some carrying lighted lamps, some with fans, some with cups filled with wine. They were still sleepy and heavy-eyed and had not yet bathed or put on fresh clothes, because Rávana was impatient to see Sita. Hánuman hid himself deeper among the leaves, for, brave as he was, he was struck with awe when he beheld Rávana.

"What splendor, what power, what majesty!" he thought. "If he were not evil, he could protect the three worlds and the gods themselves. Yet instead he is hated by all creatures."

Rávana looked down upon Sita. Though her beauty

was dimmed by sorrow, she was still radiant in her dignity and steadfastness. He flattered her and told her that
she need have no fear of him, for he truly loved her and
that the world would be hers if she would be his queen.
"What can you hope from Rama?" he asked. "Even if
he and his brother, on foot and with no army, could
come here, what could they do against me?"

Sita had heard all this many times. She picked up a
straw and held it between herself and Rávana. "Enjoy
your own wives, O prowler of the night," she said. "Do
not seek the faithful wife of another. I can no more leave
Rama than the sunlight can leave the sun. Send me back
to him if you wish to preserve your life and your kingdom, for otherwise you are doomed. Indeed, I believe
that you were able to steal me away only because this
evil deed would bring about your death. O vilest of demons, how can you escape from the wrath of my lord?"

Rávana looked at her furiously. "Truly, it is only because I love you that I do not slay you here and now," he
said, hissing like a snake. "For each harsh word you have
spoken, O daughter of Jánaka, you deserve a cruel death.
I shall grant you just two months more of life. If you
refuse me at their end, you shall be devoured by me."
And he strode off, smoldering with wrath, surrounded
by his women who tried in vain to win his favor.

When he had gone, the women who guarded Sita
crowded round her, asking, "Why do you not wish to
be the consort of this great king, who is descended from
the gods, whom even the sun and the moon obey? O
foolish one, why will you not live happily in the inner

apartments, where every luxury will be yours, where a hundred women will wait upon you and this mighty lord will cherish and adore you? We ask this for your own good, O lovely one."

"You ask me to do what I can never do," answered Sita, weeping, her head bowed. "I have but one lord and I live and breathe only because I believe that he will come and rescue me from your hands. If he knew where I am captive, he would destroy Rávana and burn down this great city in his wrath. I may die before he finds me, but I will never yield to Rávana."

Her words infuriated the demon women, who came close to her with angry looks and gestures. "So our great king, Rávana, is not worthy of you?" asked one. "Why do we entreat her?" said another. "Why do we not kill her at once and be rid of her?" But an older and more prudent demon held them back and said, "Do not lay hands upon the daughter of Jánaka! I had a terrible dream last night that made my hair stand on end, for it foretold the death of the demons and the triumph of Rama, her lord."

"Tell us your dream!" said the others.

"I saw an airy chariot made of ivory, drawn by a hundred white swans," said the old woman. "Rama and Lákshmana stood in it, clad in shining garments. Then I saw Sita, clothed in purest white, standing on a mountain in the midst of the sea, waiting for them; and she was united to her lord, as the sunlight is to the sun. After that I saw her rise from Rama's arms and stroke the faces of the sun and the moon with her hand. Again I

saw Rama and his brother seated on a mighty elephant
with four tusks, and Sita was mounted on another elephant, led by her lord, and they came and stood over
Lanka. Then I beheld Rávana fall headlong on the earth,
where a dark woman, clothed in red, put a rope about
his neck and dragged him to the realm of death. I beheld the lovely city of Lanka, her gateways and arches
shattered, fall into the sea!

"If this comes true and Rama knows how you have
tormented his beloved wife, he will kill you all. I find
no fault in her; she is virtuous and true to her lord; she
does not deserve the misfortunes that have befallen her,
and I believe that she will soon be delivered from them.
You would do better to console her and beg for her forgiveness."

Sita's heart was comforted by the telling of this dream.
She lifted her head and said to the women, "If this proves
true, I will protect you all and no harm will come to
you."

Hánuman had seen and heard all that had occurred
and he now knew beyond a doubt that he had found
Sita. "How can I show myself to her without frightening
her?" he thought. "No matter what shape I take she will
think me just another demon. I will speak to her of
Rama; that will make her trust me." He jumped into
the tree under which she sat and spoke to her in his
sweetest voice, from a low branch above her head. He
told her the whole story of Rama, praising him and
dwelling on all his virtues; he told her about the alliance

with Sugriva and said, "I am Sugriva's minister, the monkey Hánuman. I come to you as Rama's messenger and bring you good tidings; he is well and offers salutations to you, O divine Sita. His brother Lákshmana also bows before you and wishes you well. Trust me, O lovely one!"

Sita brushed back the hair that had fallen over her face and looked up, trying to find the speaker. Among the branches over her head she saw a delicate little monkey, clad in white raiment. "This must be a dream," she said to herself, "and yet it cannot be, for I do not sleep, from fear and sorrow. My mind must be distraught and this is an illusion; yet I see this monkey clearly. I do not believe that he is one of my tormentors, because my heart is delighted as I look upon him. Welcome, O gentle monkey," she said aloud, "and tell me all about Rama, how he looks and what he does and also about Lákshmana! If they are well, why do they not deliver me? Why does my lord not burn up the earth with his wrath? Does he care less for me because of my long absence?"

"O glorious princess, Rama does not know where you are," answered Hánuman. "He has searched and sorrowed for you ever since you were carried away. Now, as soon as I have spoken to him, he will come with a mighty army of monkeys and set you free. Take heart, O lovely one; he thinks of nothing but you. Behold this ring which he gave me so that you would trust me and know that I come from him."

Sita took the ring and gazed at it, overcome by joy. Then she listened eagerly as Hánuman told her all that had happened since Rávana stole her away, the months of anxious search and his own leap across the ocean; she asked a hundred questions and he answered them. "Now I have told you all," said Hánuman. "Your grief will soon be ended, for Rama will come and will rid the city of Lanka of all its demons. But I myself can save you, O daughter of Jánaka. I can bear you on my shoulders across the ocean, and this very day you shall behold Rama and his brother. Do not doubt me; mount upon my shoulders and I will carry you safely to him!"

Sita smiled at the thought. "How could your little body bear me so far, O lion among monkeys?"

Hánuman's pride was touched; he took on the mighty shape in which he had crossed the ocean and stood before Sita like a cloud or a wooded hill. "O mighty one, now I behold your power and know that you could indeed bear me away," she said. "But I fear that your speed would make me giddy and that I should fall into the ocean and be the prey of its monsters. Besides, these wicked ones would see us and pursue us and you could not fight them and protect me at the same time. If they took me from you they would either kill me at once or hide me so that I could never be found by my lord. Furthermore, O most excellent of the forest folk, since my heart is wholly given to Rama, I may not touch the body of anyone but him. When Rávana seized me in his arms and carried me off, I was helpless and had no control of my own body; but I could not touch you willingly. O best of monkeys, return at once and bring Rama and his beloved brother here with all speed!"

"You have spoken truly, O noble one," said Hánuman. "It was my devotion to you and to your lord that made me speak as I did, in order to bring you to him as quickly as possible. Since you cannot come with me, what token will you send to him so that he will know that I have truly seen you and spoken to you?"

"This is the best token that you could carry to my dear lord," said Sita, her eyes full of tears. "Ask him whether he remembers one day when we dwelt at the foot of Mount Chitrakuta. We had bathed and were resting near the river, when a crow came and pecked at the fruit in my hand. I drove it away, but it came back and attacked me, wounding me with its beak. He was asleep but I woke him with my cry and when he saw that I was hurt he was angry. He plucked a blade of grass and turned it into a fiery weapon which he threw at the crow. It flew hither and thither, trying to escape, but wherever it went, the shaft followed it until at last, exhausted, it fell at Rama's feet, begging for mercy. Remind him of that time, O Hánuman, and wish him happiness. Then offer obeisance to that noble prince, and brave Lákshmana, who left everything to follow his brother to the forest. Give to Sugriva, his ministers and to all the monkeys my wishes for their happiness. Say again and again to Rama, 'I have but two months to live, O destroyer of your foes! Make haste to deliver me!' Tell him of my hard and bitter suffering and all the demons' threats!" She took from her robe a jeweled band that used to bind her hair; in it was set a great pearl that adorned her forehead in happier days. She asked Hánuman to give it to Rama and he slipped it on his finger, since it was too small for his arm.

"Do not be anxious or sorrowful, O noble Queen," he said. "Soon you will see those valiant monkeys, thick as clouds, roaring upon the mountains of Lanka, fighting with their nails and teeth, like lions and tigers. Who can overcome Rama? Who can equal Lákshmana? Have patience until we come!"

Then he took leave of her, and, first bowing low with joined palms, he walked around her thrice, keeping her on his right.

13

Hanuman Sets Lanka on Fire

Hánuman was triumphant because he had succeeded in his mission. "A truly able messenger not only fulfills his chief purpose but does even more," he thought. "If I can return to Sugriva and tell him how strong and numerous these demons are, the information will be helpful to him. I will lay waste this garden and surely Rávana will send out his whole army against me and then I can see it."

He took his most powerful shape and raged like a tempest through that lovely grove, uprooting trees, shattering the pavilions where the ladies of the court were wont to rest, terrifying the birds and the gentle animals, who fled, crying out, in all directions. He spared the part where Sita was, but the rest he laid in ruins. Then he stood at the gate, blazing with wrath. The women

who guarded Sita ran into the palace and told Rávana
that a gigantic ape was ruining the ashoka grove. He
sent forth his guards, armed with every sort of weapon,
and they rushed upon Hánuman as moths fly to a flame.
Filled with power and courage, he lashed his tail and
roared, "Victory to Rama and Lákshmana and to Sugriva,
king of the monkeys! I am Hánuman, son of the Storm-
God, destroyer of my foes!" He picked up an iron bar
that lay by the gate and laid about him right and left,
slaying the guards, who were already terrified by his
roaring and his size, for he stood above them like a
thundercloud.

A few escaped him and went back to tell their king
what had befallen them. Rávana, his eyes rolling with
fury, sent forth his son who had never been defeated;
indeed, he had overcome Indra himself, god of gods, and
taken him captive; he was therefore known as Indrajita,
or conqueror of Indra. This mighty warrior came forth
in his chariot, armed with his great bow, whose string
he twanged with a sound like thunder. Hánuman leapt
hither and thither, avoiding the fierce arrows of Indrajita, and neither one was able to take the other unawares
or to break through his defenses.

Finally, Indrajita used a divine weapon, given him by
Brahma. He loosed it and it wrapped itself about the
monkey's body, making him powerless. Hánuman fell
to the ground without a struggle, for he knew that he
was bound by a divine force and was helpless. "Let them
take me to Rávana," he thought, "I wish to meet him
face to face before I leave." Indrajita's soldiers came for-

ward and bound him with hempen rope, for they could
not see the divine bonds. As soon as they had done this,
Hánuman was freed from the Brahma weapon, for it
lost its power as soon as other means were used. Nonetheless he allowed himself to be dragged into the court
by the soldiers, who struck him with their fists. They
brought him before Rávana, who sat on his throne like
a blazing sun in his might and glory.

"Who is this and whence has he come?" asked some
of the courtiers. "Kill him! Burn him! Devour him!"
cried others.

"Ask this perverse wretch why he laid waste my grove
and killed my guards," said Rávana, his eyes red with
fury. "Whence comes he and why has he entered this
city?"

"I have come from Sugriva, lord of all the monkeys, O
mighty King," answered Hánuman fearlessly. "He
salutes you as a brother and, as a brother, sends you this
counsel. It is not fitting for you, who knows what is right
and lawful, to bear away another's wife. This act will
lead to your ruin. It is not Sita whom you hold captive
in your garden; it is a five-headed serpent, a cup of poison,
the very noose of death. No one can stand against the
wrath of Rama and of Lákshmana, O King. You believe
that no god or demon can slay you; Sugriva is neither
god nor demon, and Rama is a man. Ponder these words,
O mighty one, and restore Sita to her lord, that lion
among men!"

Rávana, his anger increased by this bold and unwelcome speech, ordered his soldiers to put Hánuman to death.

Now Rávana had a younger brother, Vibíshana, who was wiser than he and knew the path of virtue. He, too, had fasted and disciplined himself as Rávana had done a long time ago; but when Brahma offered him a boon, he had asked that his mind be ever fixed on righteousness, no matter what might befall him. He now spoke quietly to his brother, "Control your anger, O conqueror of foes, and remember that a messenger must never be put to death! He speaks for those who sent him and it is they who must be slain. Let him return to the two proud princes whose envoy he is, so that they may come here and meet their death."

"You speak truly," answered Rávana. "I will not slay him, but I will punish him. Monkeys value their tails above all else; therefore set his tail on fire and lead him through the city! Then let him return to his friends disgraced and disfigured."

The soldiers wrapped the end of Hánuman's tail with cotton rags soaked in oil and then set them on fire, while all the assemblage laughed and made fun of him. He lashed at them with his burning tail but did not free himself, for he thought, "Now I shall see the whole city and its fortifications by daylight, having seen it before by night." The demons paraded him through the city, announcing his misdeeds with conch shells and trumpets. Hánuman looked at every street and house so keenly that his guards believed him to be a spy, as indeed he was.

The women who guarded Sita ran back to her and

told her that the great monkey had his tail set ablaze, and Sita silently prayed to Agni, God of Fire, that he would not burn Hánuman or hurt him. And Hánuman, led by the soldiers along the streets of Lanka, wondered why his burning tail gave him no pain. "Surely the God of Fire favors me for Sita's and Rama's sakes," he thought. "Now why should I let myself be led about by these vile fiends? It is time for me to avenge myself!"

He broke his fetters and with a shout leaped upon the gate of the city. He took a small form and shook off the remaining ropes and looked about him. "What more can I do to make these demons unhappy?" he said to himself. "I will set their city ablaze with the flame that they themselves have lighted."

He leaped along the roofs from palace to palace, everywhere lashing out with his fiery tail and leaving flames behind him. As he went he shouted, "Victory to Rama and to King Sugriva! I am their messenger; I am Hánuman, son of the wind!" Shrieks arose from those mansions as the wind fanned the flames and they spread from one building to another. Hánuman was delighted at the mischief he had created and frolicked about the great city, setting fires everywhere and examining carefully its walls and fortifications. Then he sat down on a high tower and looked about him, seeing the flames rising on all sides and hearing the demons' cries of distress. The rays of his burning tail made a sort of halo about him as he sat there, well satisfied with his work. Then he leaped down to the seashore and swung his tail into the cool water to quench the fire.

His anger cooled at the same time; he thought of Sita and suddenly was horrified by a fear that she might have been hurt by the flames that he had started. "Alas, what evil have I done?" he thought. "Happy are those great souls who conquer their anger, as fire is quenched by water. What if Sita has been injured, or even killed? All would be lost: Rama would die if she died, and so would Lákshmana, and then Bhárata and Shátrughna could bear to live no longer. Maybe her virtue has kept her safe. I must make sure."

He took the shape of an ordinary monkey and bounded through the smoking city to the ashoka grove, where Sita still sat, holding Rama's ring and thinking of all that Hánuman and the demon women had said. He bowed to her, saying, "By the grace of heaven you are not harmed, O goddess."

She was delighted to see him again. "O Hánuman, my child, can you not stay in some hidden spot, only for today?" she pleaded. "Take some rest and then set out tomorrow! It is a great comfort to me to see you, and I do not know whether I shall live till you return. When you go, I shall be drowned again in fear and sorrow. Tell me, how can that host of brave monkeys, and my lord and his brother, cross the impassable ocean, as you alone were able to do?"

"Do not fear, gentle lady," answered Hánuman. "The chief of all the forest folk, Sugriva, has sworn to deliver you and has summoned all the monkeys in the world to carry out his vow. There are many as powerful as I am; the best are never chosen to go on a dangerous mission.

You shall soon see Rama strike Rávana to the earth with his arrows, and he will bear you away to Ayodhya and end all your sorrow. Take heart, dear Mother!" He made obeisance to her and left her. He was eager now to return with his good tidings and to see his companions and Sugriva and Rama again.

Hánuman scrambled up the nearest mountain and gathered up his strength, this time with joy and assurance, whereas before he had leapt across the ocean not knowing what he might find or if he would ever return. Pressing down the mountain with his feet and hands, he shot into the air like an arrow loosed from the bow. He clove the clouds and drank the sky, coursing on and on until he saw the northern shore and that mountain from which he had leapt on his southern journey. When he beheld it, eager to see his friends again, he waved his tail to and fro and filled the sky with his roars.

The monkeys on the shore had waited anxiously for him. Now they knew from his shouts that he had succeeded in his quest, and, mad with joy, they bounded up the mountainside to meet him. Climbing to the tops of the trees, they stripped off their upper garments and waved them in the air, and when he alighted, they crowded round him, their faces shining with joy. They brought a leafy branch for him to sit upon and fruits to refresh him.

Hánuman bowed to his elders and to Angada and then said, "I have seen Sita!" The monkeys shouted and leaped about him, waving their tails.

"You are the bravest and strongest of us all, O Hánu-

man, since you have crossed the immeasurable ocean
and come back victorious," said Angada. "You have
given us back our lives, for now we can return to Rama
and Sugriva."

Then the others quieted down and sat around Hánuman, their eyes fixed on him, to hear his story. He told
them everything that had happened from the time that
he had left them and said at last, "Now it is for you to
carry out what is still to be done so that Sita may be
restored to her lord. She is nearly worn out with grief
and terror and has but two months to live. I alone have
entered Lanka; I have killed many demons and set fire
to the city. How much more could be done by all of us
together!"

"Why must such brave warriors as we are wait for
those who are still in Kishkindha?" said Angada. "I
alone can destroy the city of Lanka and Rávana himself.
Hánuman has already begun their destruction; let us
finish it and bring Sita back ourselves!" The oldest and
wisest of the monkeys, whom Sugriva had sent to advise
Angada, answered him sensibly, "We were told by Sugriva and Rama to explore the southern region and to
find Sita, but we were not told to bring her back, O son
of Bali, nor would Rama be pleased if we did so, for he
has vowed to rescue her himself and to kill Rávana.
Therefore let us return and tell them the result of our
quest and lay the matter before them."

All the others, including Angada, approved of this
speech and ran down the mountain, eager to return to
Kishkindha. They were proud of themselves because of

their success, eager to tell their good news, and sure of victory. Jumping and frisking, chattering and swinging through the trees, they covered the distance quickly, no longer having to stop and search in every direction as they had done on their southward journey.

Just before they arrived at Kishkindha they came to a beautiful pleasure garden belonging to Sugriva. None might enter it without his consent and guards were posted around it. It was a honey garden, and within it were beautiful flowers and trees beloved by the bees; at this season the branches were heavy with fruit and honeycombs, and there were quiet pools covered with lilies and lotuses.

The monkeys longed to enter the grove and asked Angada's permission. He agreed, and they dashed in like a torrent, throwing themselves into the trees, breaking down the branches as they stripped them of their fruits and honeycombs. They drank the honey and threw away the combs. Some pressed the wax into balls and threw them at each other; some broke leafy boughs and lay down on them to sleep; others chased each other round the trees, laughing and shouting. Some of them fought playfully, rolling on the ground, biting and scratching; some sang at the top of their voices, and others imitated the voices of different animals, roaring like lions or whistling like birds. They chattered ceaselessly, none listening to any other, for they were drunk with honey and full of joy and pride.

The guards, hearing and seeing all this uproar and destruction, set upon the roisterers and tried to drive

them out; but the intruders, led by Hánuman and
Angada, threw them back and knocked them down. For
Hánuman was as excited as any of them. "Take all the
honey you want!" he shouted. "I will drive away anyone who tries to stop you." Angada laughed and said,
"Do whatever Hánuman tells you to do, even if it is
wrong. It is he who has saved us."

The guards fled, but their leader ran to Sugriva, who
was sitting with Rama and Lákshmana beside the cave
where those heroes lived. He bowed, touching Sugriva's
feet, and told him how his monkeys, led by Hánuman,
were destroying the grove.

"They would never have done such a thing if they
had not succeeded in their mission," said Sugriva to
Rama. "Hánuman must have found Sita, for he alone
could do so. Besides, the month is more than past; they
would hardly dare to return at all if they had not been
successful. O Rama, Sita must have been found!

"I am delighted that those heroes have eaten the fruit
and honey," he said to the guardian of the grove.
"We must be patient with the naughtiness of those who
bring us victory. Return now and send them to me at
once!"

When he returned, the guardian found all the monkeys resting happily on the grass or among the branches
of the trees. He begged their pardon for having fought
against them and gave them Sugriva's message, telling
them that their king was not at all angry with them but
was pleased.

So they all started home again, excited and happy,

Hánuman's Tail on Fire

and their cries and shouts were heard long before they arrived and flung themselves at the feet of Sugriva and Rama. Hánuman, his hands joined palm to palm, said to Rama, "I have found Sita and spoken with her." He took from his finger the jeweled band that held the great pearl that Sita had entrusted to him and gave it to Rama who, with his brother, gazed at it with eyes full of tears.

"This pearl was given to Sita by her father on our wedding day," said Rama. "O Hánuman, tell me again and again all that my gentle, sweet-spoken, and beautiful princess said to you. How can she bear her life among those grim and fearful fiends? Now tell me everything!"

14

The Advance on Lanka

The two brothers, Sugriva, and that whole assemblage of monkeys listened spellbound while Hánuman told his story. "No one but Hánuman could have carried out so hard and dangerous a task," said Rama when he finished. "What courage and what power! I wish that I had any fitting reward to give him! This is all that I can do." And he clasped the monkey to him in a close embrace.

"Now let us depart, O Sugriva," he said, turning to that great king. "All the favorable stars are rising and we shall be victorious. Let a guard of the strongest and bravest of your troops go ahead to explore the way and to lead us through woods where fruit, honey, and fresh water may be found. Let them send scouts into ravines and thickets to see that there is no enemy ambush. I myself, mounted upon the shoulders of Hánuman, and Lákshmana, riding on those of Angada, like the gods on their celestial elephants, will march in the center, while the wise and mighty elders protect the rear."

Sugriva called to all the monkeys, and they came leaping and shouting from the caves and mountainsides. Those who had searched for Sita in the north, east, and west had all returned within the month's time with nothing accomplished; now, with their purpose made clear and a glorious battle ahead of them, they assembled in a moment and were ready to start, while those who had gone with Hánuman considered themselves the leaders and went bounding on ahead. All of them were in high spirits, turning handsprings and playing leapfrog as they went. They avoided cities and public roads, keeping to the woods where they always found their favorite food and plenty of water. They surged ahead, a very ocean of monkeys, raising a great cloud of dust and covering the earth. They rested by lakes and rivers, passed over forested mountains and across plains, full of joy and running like the wind. Rama and Lákshmana rode high and swiftly on the shoulders of their friends, happy to be off at last, after the long months of waiting.

"When you have slain Rávana and freed Sita, we shall return to Ayodhya, for the years of our exile will be over," said Lákshmana. "Everywhere I see favorable omens, O King of men: a fresh wind follows us, the sun shines clear, the star of our dynasty gleams brightly while that of the demons is in a bad position, there is plenty of

fruit and sweet water and the trees are flowering out of
season. How splendid is this army of monkeys!"

"When I have put those demons to flight and my shafts
have pierced the breast of Rávana, Sita will live anew as
the autumn moon shines forth again after the rain clouds
have gone," answered Rama.

At last they reached the shore of the ocean and Sugriva
ordered the whole army to encamp there, where it
looked like another, tawny-colored, ocean. Their chatter
as they gazed and wondered at those limitless waters
was louder than the thunder of the waves. The leaders
of the army with Rama and Lákshmana met to take
counsel together.

"How shall we and this mighty army cross the ocean,
O chief of the forest rangers?" asked Rama. "Only
Hánuman, Angada and you are able to leap across it.
Unless there is a bridge to carry us, Lanka can never be
reached."

"There stands Nala, O my friend," answered Sugriva.
"He is the son of the architect of the gods who built
Lanka itself; he has his father's skill and power. He will
build a bridge for us." Nala came forward with joined
hands. "I have not spoken of my powers, since no one
asked me concerning them," he said. "I can build a
causeway over the Sea-God's domain, if all the army will
help me."

Rama rejoiced and ordered the monkeys to do whatever Nala desired. Under his orders they dashed up the
mountainside and began to tear down mighty trees and
rocks, rolling or pushing them down the hill or flinging

them into the sea with a mighty splash. Hundreds and thousands of them rushed hither and thither, some uprooting the trees and loosing great blocks of stone, others moving them to the shore where hundreds more put them in place just as Nala told them to do. The great causeway, on the second day, began to stretch out across the sea.

At this same time Rávana was holding a council in Lanka. He sat on his splendid throne, surrounded by his warriors, his ministers, his brothers, and his sons. He had many brothers, some of whom joined him in his evil deeds, as Khara did, whom Rama had slain in the Dándaka forest. Others held aloof or tried to hold him back, for all of them were learned in the Vedas and knew the path of virtue, whether or not they followed it. Rávana's eldest brother, whom he had driven out of Lanka, had mounted his airy chariot, fashioned by the same divine architect who had built his city, and had traveled far to the north and taken up his abode in the Himalaya mountains. The gods had made him guardian of all the treasure of the earth; he was Kúvera, God of Wealth. Yet Rávana had pursued him even there and had robbed him of the marvelous chariot, which he coveted.

Now, in his council hall, a younger brother sat next to him; his name was Kumbhakarna and he was of immense size and terrifying to behold. He ate so much that the gods feared that he might devour every living thing; therefore they had condemned him to sleep his life away,

waking only twice a year for a single day, to keep himself alive. This was one of his waking moments. Next to
him sat Vibíshana, who had saved Hánuman's life and
was deeply troubled because of his brother's wickedness,
especially the carrying away of Sita. Near them were
other brothers and Rávana's sons, foremost among them
Indrajita, powerful and arrogant.

Although he blazed with glory and was surrounded
by these mighty warriors and counselors, Rávana's heart
was heavy. "Our great fortified city has been set on fire
and turned upside down by a mere monkey," he said to
them, "and now my spies tell me that Rama, surrounded
by a host of heroic apes, has reached the northern shore
of the ocean. What should I do now? Tell me what you
think the best plan for me to adopt."

The leaders of his army gave him bad advice, for they
were very proud. "Have you not defeated all your enemies, O King—gods, demons and those great serpents,
the Nagas?" said one. "Have you not mounted into the
sky and descended into the depths of the ocean and
always come forth victorious? It is not worthy of you to
fear a crowd of apes led by a mere man. Send forth your
son Indrajita and he will destroy them all!"

"We had been feasting and most of us were drunk
when that impudent monkey took us by surprise and
deceived us with his tricks," said another. "As long as I
live that ranger of the woods shall never return here
alive." "What does that puny and miserable monkey
matter?" cried another, brandishing his great mace. "It
is Rama, his brother, and Sugriva whom we must de-

stroy. Give me leave, my lord, to kill them all today, singlehanded, with my mace!" So they boasted, one after another, until they were all on their feet, shouting and brandishing their weapons.

Then Vibíshana rose and begged them to be seated. He spoke quietly to his brother: "It is foolish to belittle Rama, O vanquisher of your foes. He has tremendous forces at his disposal; he is in the right, for he always follows the path of virtue, and you will not be able to defeat him. What wrong has he done to you, O prowler of the night, that you should go to his retreat and carry off his wife? If he slew our brother and his host in the forest, he did so in self-defense. It is because you stole Sita away that we are now in great danger. Give her back to him before he destroys this city with all its defenders; give her back to him at once and let us live here happily with our wives and children! Everyone in your court knows that you are in the wrong, O lord of demons, but they dare not speak truly to you. I alone, your brother, dare to speak for your own good!"

"I shall never give her up!" answered Rávana angrily. "I brought her here from the Dándaka forest and here she will stay until she yields to my desire. I have never seen anyone to compare with her in beauty; when I look upon her I am no longer master of myself. It is not for us to return her to her lord, but to kill Rama and his brother, and then she will yield to me. Even if they were upheld by the gods, how could they stand against me?"

"Ever since you first saw Sita your mind has been possessed by her as a lake is filled by the waters of a river," said Kumbhakarna scornfully. "This is not worthy of you, O great King. You should have asked our advice at the beginning of this affair, not at the end. You did this evil deed without forethought and are lucky that Rama did not slay you as you did it. Nevertheless, O unconquerable one, now that it is done I shall stand by you. I shall destroy Rama, his brother, and all those monkeys, and drink their blood."

"Why are you so fearful, O youngest of my uncles?" said Indrajita to Vibíshana. "No other demon would speak as you have spoken. Are you alone lacking in courage and strength and daring? Who are these two sons of a mortal king? Have I not humbled the pride of the gods themselves; am I not able to slay these two, who are but men?"

"It is only because the fierce arrows from Rama's bow have not pierced your limbs that you can boast so," answered Vibíshana. "Neither Rávana nor his brothers nor all his sons can overcome Rama in battle. Yet all of you flatter him and lead him to destruction. Under the guise of a dutiful son you are really your father's enemy, since you support him in his evil doing; you should instead save him, even by dragging him back by the hair of his head from this enterprise. I say again, O my brother, give Sita back to Rama with treasure and jewels and rich attire!"

"It is better to live with a venomous serpent than with an enemy who poses as a friend," said Rávana harshly. "The worst danger we face is from our own kin, as those elephants know who are captured in the forest with the help of tamed elephants. If any other had spoken to me as you have spoken, he would have died where he stood. As for you, a curse upon you, O disgrace of our family!"

Vibíshana rose to his feet, mace in hand, and four of his friends rose with him. "You have lost your reason, my brother," he said. "At the point of death a doomed man refuses medicine. I have spoken because I could not bear to see you caught in the snare of death, but you will not listen. Farewell, O King. You will be happier without me." He left the court and his four friends followed him. When they came out of the palace gate, they rose into the air and proceeded at once to the northern shore of the ocean where Rama and his army were encamped.

Sugriva was standing on the shore with Hánuman and a few other companions when he saw Vibíshana and his friends coming over the ocean, their weapons and jewels flashing in the sun. "Surely these armed demons are coming to kill us," he said.

"Let us slay them at once, O King!" answered the monkeys, and they rushed off to uproot trees and lift up stones as weapons.

Vibíshana alighted at a little distance from them and said, "I am the younger brother of Rávana, that wicked king who carried off Sita; my name is Vibíshana. I have tried to make him return Sita to her lord, but he would not listen and cursed me. So I have left him, my wife and children, and all my possessions, and come hither to take refuge with Rama. Pray tell him that I have come."

Sugriva hastened to Rama, gave him the message and said, "This must be a spy of Rávana, who has sent him here to find out our plans and our weak points. He is a demon and a brother of our enemy. How can we trust him? Let us put him to death!"

Rama asked the advice of the other leaders. "Let us be on our guard against him," said one. "If he has abandoned his brother, whom else might he betray?"

"We should not trust him immediately," said Angada. "Let us examine him carefully before we decide on anything."

"When anyone is questioned, he answers carefully or perhaps will not answer at all, if he is wise," said Hánuman. "The character of another person is known only through much talk and acquaintance. I find no fault in this demon; his face is honest and his speech is clear; he is not embarrassed and does not seem guilty. He knows the wickedness of Rávana and your greatness of heart, Lord Rama. I think that his coming here proves his worth. It is for you to decide, O wisest of men."

"I shall never refuse anyone who presents himself as a friend," said Rama. "Even a villain who comes with joined palms, asking for refuge, should not be turned away, and those who throw themselves on the mercy of their enemy should be protected by him. Bring this stranger to me, O monkeys; he shall be safe even if it is Rávana himself."

Vibíshana came, knelt at Rama's feet and touched them, as did his four friends. "I have come to seek refuge with you, O protector of the world," he said. "I have left Lanka and all I possess to place my life and happiness at your disposal."

Rama looked searchingly at him and said, "Tell me truly, O Vibíshana, what is the strength and what is the weakness of Rávana?" Vibíshana described the whole extent of his brother's power, the number of his forces, the qualities of his foremost warriors. Hánuman had already described the city and its fortifications.

Rama listened carefully and then said, "No matter what his power and that of his generals, I shall slay Rávana and all his sons and kinsmen. If he plunges into the ocean depths or takes refuge in heaven he will not escape me. Then I shall crown you king of Lanka, O Vibíshana. Until this is done I shall not return to Ayodhya; I swear it by my three brothers!"

"I will help you with all my power," answered Vibíshana, and they embraced one another, in the presence of the monkeys, who shouted with joy as they beheld that powerful ally who knew all the strength and the secrets of their enemy.

The causeway was quickly built under Nala's direction. The whole mountainside was torn down, its trees and rocks forming the foundation, its stones and earth filling in the cracks. The monkeys rushed back and forth along it, carrying the materials, growing more and more excited as it approached the shore of the island. All things helped them: the winds were quiet and the ocean calmed itself and held the bridge steady, its waves lapping gently against the sides. Finally it was done and lay across the quiet water like the parting of a woman's hair. It was so strong and well built that the remains of it and many of the great rocks that the monkeys threw down can still be seen today.

Rama and Lákshmana mounted on the shoulders of their friends, and the whole army began to move across. Some of the monkeys marched along the causeway; others dived into the waves; some sprang into the sky in their joy. When the leaders arrived on the shore of Lanka, they decided to encamp for the night, and they waited there until the rest of that great horde arrived, for it took a long time for them all to cross over.

The next morning all the armies were marshaled and arranged in order, each with its leaders, and they set out at once for Lanka. As they advanced they beheld a mountain with three peaks and the glittering city on its summit. Facing it and nearer to them was another mountain, and Rama decided to camp on its slope, whence he could examine Lanka and its defenses. They all climbed up, the monkeys scrambling and bounding to the top in no time, and from its height they looked at the vast extent of those golden walls, the high gates, the innumerable palaces rising like sunlit clouds above their blossoming groves.

"What a marvelous city!" said Rama to his brother. "It was built by a god and seems to touch the skies. And there my Sita is held captive, thin and pale with grief, lying on the bare ground! She will be frightened when she hears the clamor of war." The monkeys, too, were amazed but not dismayed. "We shall destroy Lanka with the peaks of its own mountain, or if need be, with our bare fists!" they cried, and roared their defiance.

Meanwhile Rávana had heard of the building of the causeway, which amazed him, and of the great army that was already on his shores. He sent out two trusted spies, ordering them to find out the exact number of the enemy, their strength, and the weapons used by Rama and Lákshmana. The two spies took the shape of monkeys and joined that great host, but they could not begin to count the vast number that swarmed over the hills and plains, while the power and the roars of those great apes made their hair stand on end. They were not noticed by anyone except Vibíshana; he saw through their disguise and had them seized and brought before Rama. They were terrified and joined the palms of their hands in supplication. "O mighty prince, we were sent by Rávana to find out the size and the strength of your army," said one of them.

"If you have already found out all that you want to know, return in peace," answered Rama, smiling. "If there is anything else you wish to investigate, Vibíshana will show it to you. Do not fear: you are envoys and will not be harmed. When you return, say these words to your king in my name: 'Come forth and fight against me, O vilest of demons! Put forth all your strength and valor! You will not escape me though you search the three worlds for refuge. My dreadful wrath will fall upon you at dawn tomorrow, O Rávana!'"

The spies paid obeisance to him and returned in haste to Lanka. They gave Rávana the message and told him that Rama alone could overthrow the city and that it was useless to fight against him.

"What enemy can overthrow me, the lord of the demons, the terror of the gods?" asked Rávana arrogantly. "Show me these monkeys and their leaders!" He led them up into a tower of his palace, and looking forth, he saw the whole earth covered with that enormous and invincible army.

The spies pointed out each leader with his followers. "Each one of them vows that he will destroy this city, O King. They lash their tails and grind their teeth with fury against you; they are brave and ferocious and eager to fight; their roars alone will shatter these walls. We could not count them any more than we could count the sands of the seashore. These warriors, O King, are born of the gods and of the musicians and dancers of heaven and can change their shape at will.

"Behold those that stand there in the center! That one, as tall as an elephant, is he who crossed the ocean and set the city on fire. Do you not recognize him? He believes that he can destroy Lanka singlehanded. Next to him is that warrior, dark-skinned and large-eyed, whose heroism is known in the three worlds, who never swerves from righteousness. That is Rama who has come to war with you, O King. On his right, radiant as gold refined in fire, is Lákshmana, his brother and second self. On his left is your own brother, Vibíshana, whom Rama will make king of Lanka; he, too, has come to fight you! That other mighty one, standing near them like a rock, rules over all the monkeys and dwells in Kishkindha, a great citadel hewn from the mountain. He wears a golden chain bestowed by Indra. The chain and the kingdom he owes to Rama and has come hither to repay his debt. Powerful is the army that follows him, O mighty King! Before it attacks, return Sita to her lord!"

"Have you no fear of death that you speak so insolently to me?" asked Rávana furiously. "Begone and leave me!" He called his ministers together and said to them, "Beat the drums, sound the trumpets, and call all my forces together!" Then, with his generals, he planned the defense of his city, setting at each gate an army commanded by a great warrior, and taking the northern gate himself.

Sita was sitting forlornly, her head bowed, in that grove where the demon women guarded her, when she heard the uproar of drums, gongs, and trumpets. She started up in fear, but Vibíshana's wife, Sarama, who was as good as he, had become her friend and hastened to her now to comfort her.

"Do not fear, O blessed one," she said. "I have good news for you. Rama has crossed the ocean with a mighty army and is besieging the city. The clamor that you hear is made by the troops that Rávana has called forth. Rama will slay him in battle and take you back to Ayodhya, O lovely one. Soon you will be united to your lord and will be weeping tears of joy. He will loosen your hair from the braid that has bound it for so many months and you will cast off your sorrow as a snake sloughs off its skin. Now tell me what I can do for you, for I can change my shape at will and fly through the air at your behest."

"May happiness attend you!" answered Sita. "I wish to know what Rávana intends to do. I tremble with fear of him, for he threatens and insults me continually. If there is any talk in the assembly of freeing me or of keeping me captive, pray let me know it, O kind Sarama!"

Her friend went back into the palace and soon returned to Sita. "Rávana's mother has sent word to him that he must restore you with honor to your lord," she said. "She says that Rama's astonishing deed in the forest, when he slew the demon host, should be a lesson to the king. A wise old counselor has told him the same thing. But that wicked wretch will never give you up any more than a miser will give up his gold. When Rama has slain him you will be free at last, O daughter of Jánaka!"

Rama, Lákshmana, and their friends also heard the clamor that arose in Lanka, and they planned their attack. Vibíshana said, "My four friends have already been to Lanka and have returned. They changed their shapes and examined everything that Rávana is doing. Hear them, O mighty one!" The demons told Rama how Rávana had defended the gates and that he himself was stationed at the north. Then Rama appointed four armies to attack each gate, with great warriors to lead each one.

"It is my right to kill that wicked king; therefore I shall force the northern gate," he said. "Let the monkeys keep their own shapes so that we may not confuse them with the enemy. Only seven of us will be in human form: Lákshmana and I, Vibíshana and his four companions."

Then, the time having come, Rama descended the mountain, inspected his armies, and gave the signal to

The March Across the Causeway

advance. Joyously and exultantly, bow in hand, he and Lákshmana and their allies set out for Lanka, followed by that great host. The monkeys, though they wore clothes and lived in houses, had no weapons except rocks and the strong branches of trees, as well as their powerful fists, as hard as stones, and their nails and teeth which were like those of tigers. They armed themselves on the mountainside.

Soon they all came beneath the mighty walls of the city, topped with banners and guarded by innumerable soldiers. Each leader took his army to the gate allotted to him and the monkeys awaited eagerly the signal to attack, trembling with excitement, lashing their tails with fury. The demons, looking down upon that sea of hostile apes, were amazed and terrified; their hearts were heavy because they knew of the wicked deed their king had committed.

15

The Battle

At Rama's command, the monkeys, in hundreds and thousands, rushed upon the mountain that upheld Lanka and began to scale its heights, roaring like thunderclouds. They tore down the outposts and reached the foot of the walls. Then Rávana ordered his troops to attack, and they poured out of the gates like the winds that will sweep the earth at doomsday. With the banging of kettledrums, the blare of trumpets and conch shells, they came forth in chariots and on elephants and horses, clad in mail and armed with every sort of weapon.

An appalling battle began between them, the monkeys yelling, "Victory to Rama and Sugriva!" the demons shouting, "Glory to Rávana!" Although the demons were better armed, they were surprised and confused by

the attacks of the monkeys, who could smash a chariot
and kill its horses with one sweep of the huge branches
they carried, or with their great rocks. Often they
avoided the arrows and the lances of the foe by leaping
upon the demons and crushing them in their powerful
arms, biting them or scratching their eyes out. One blow
of the palms of their hands or their fists could kill any
creature. Rama and Lákshmana sent forth clouds of
arrows from their bows, destroying the arrows of the
enemy bowmen and slaying numberless soldiers.

At the end of that first day, apes and demons, horses
and elephants lay dead upon the field among broken
chariots, swords, shields, and fallen banners. The monkeys, trusting in Rama and Lákshmana, were weary but
triumphant, while the demons longed for the coming of
the night that would put an end to the battle.

On the next day and the following days Rávana sent
forth his best warriors, ordering each one to kill Rama
and Lákshmana. Every day one of them was slain in
single combat, sometimes by Hánuman, sometimes by
Angada who, though young, was a mighty warrior, then
by Sugriva, after a fierce and terrible fight. Meanwhile
all around them monkeys and demons fought and many
on both sides were slain and many sorely wounded. The
forest folk were used to wielding great branches or even
young trees, and they soon picked up maces and swords
that had fallen from the hands of dead warriors and used
them well. Victory came on one day to one side and the
next day to the other; sometimes the monkeys fled in
terror before a fierce attack and again it was the night-

prowlers who sought the shelter of the city's walls. At night, in Rama's camp, after the wounded had been cared for, those heroic fighters who had killed a great enemy in single combat were praised and acclaimed by their leaders and companions, while the demons returned to their city downcast and silent.

Rávana's fury and his anxiety increased as his warriors were killed. When his chief general, the leader of his army, had fallen under the monkeys' blows, he decided to waken Kumbhakarna, who was a mighty warrior, in spite of his fatness and his enormous appetite; he had often fought beside Rávana in his wars against the gods. He was now fast asleep in a cavern on the side of the mountain, and Rávana sent soldiers to waken him.

First they gathered together huge quantities of food and drink, for they knew that the first thing he would want was an enormous meal; they took also garlands and perfumes to please him. All these they carried to the cave where they found him fast asleep, lying full length upon a couch. They shouted at him and blew conch shells and trumpets; they banged on drums and gongs and raised such an uproar that the birds, flying by, fell down from the sky. But nothing roused Kumbhakarna and his snoring was louder than all the noise they made. At last the soldiers climbed upon his body and jumped up and down upon it, and Kumbhakarna opened his huge mouth and yawned and then sat up, his eyes heavy with sleep.

"Why have you awakened me?" he asked. "Is the king in danger?" They told him what had happened

since he sat in Rávana's council hall: how Rama and his
army had crossed the ocean and were besieging Lanka
and that Rávana had called for him. He ate first all that
they had brought to him; then he went to the city and
to his brother's palace, making the earth tremble under
his steps.

He bowed to the king of demons and asked him why
he had been awakened. "You have slept long and do not
know the danger we are in from Rama and his host of
invincible monkeys. They are destroying us all," answered Rávana. "The city is besieged and hard pressed;
the best of our warriors have been killed, and I do not
know how these rangers of the wood can be defeated.
Save us, O scourge of your foes! All our hopes are placed
on you."

Kumbhakarna gave a mocking laugh. "Swift punishment has come upon you for the misdeed which we all
condemned," he said. "But do not fear, since I am here.
I will strike down Rama and his brother today and
eat up all these contemptible apes. Let your army rest;
I shall go forth alone. Drink your wine and banish grief;
I will bring you victory."

"Go forth with well-armed troops!" commanded
Rávana. "You do not know how fierce and brave these
monkeys are. Anyone rash enough to meet them alone
will be torn to pieces by them." He stepped down from
his throne and placed a splendid diadem on Kumbhakarna's head and adorned him with a jeweled necklace
and earrings. Then that great demon armed himself,
and surrounded by soldiers on elephants, horses, and

chariots, he went forth from the gate on foot, towering over them all because of his great size.

When he emerged from the gate and saw that vast army before him, he shouted with a voice like a thunder-clap and the monkeys fled in all directions, smitten with fear, some of them running back even to the causeway by which they had come. Their leaders called to them and rallied them, and Angada, that fearless and mighty warrior, hurled himself upon the huge fiend, striking him with a rock. Hánuman and Sugriva followed him, but they were all struck senseless by the blows of the demon's mace. Then the monkeys fled to Rama for help, and Kumbhakarna followed them and came face to face with the two brothers.

Lákshmana challenged him, loosing a flight of arrows that could not pierce the golden armor of his foe, who passed him by. "Go hence, O Lákshmana," he said. "I wish to meet Rama. When I have slain him I will fight you."

"Behold him yonder, standing like a rock, O mighty warrior!" said Lákshmana with a mocking smile, and the demon rushed furiously upon Rama. He whirled his great mace but Rama, with an arrow, cut off the arm that held it. With the other arm the fiend picked up a tree that the monkeys had dropped and came roaring on, and Rama pierced that arm. Then he chose one of the celestial weapons, an arrow whose shaft was inlaid with gold and jewels, brilliant as flame, swift as a thunderbolt. It struck off Kumbhakarna's enormous head, which fell with its diadem and its swinging earrings, while the shock of his fall made the earth tremble. The monkeys leaped up with radiant faces when they saw him fall, and his followers fled, wailing, to the gates.

When Rávana heard of Kumbhakarna's death, he wept with grief and rage. Nonetheless, he had brothers left, and sons. Next day he sent forth four of his young sons, guarded by two of his brothers and a host of warriors. They went on splendid chariots, on war horses, and elephants, their brows crowned with diadems, their banners flying, to the sound of drums and gongs.

The monkeys were encouraged by their victories, and met this company eagerly, shouting their defiance, brandishing their weapons. And one by one, Rávana's sons and brothers were slain. One was killed by a blow of Angada's fist, another by Hánuman, a third by a rock hurled by Nala, the builder of the causeway. Still another was killed by Hánuman with his own sword which the monkey wrested from his hand. In the same way one of Rávana's brothers was struck down by his own mace brandished by a great ape. The last and most powerful of the king's four sons, who rode on a chariot filled with spears and darts and quivers of arrows, drove the monkeys aside and challenged Rama or Lákshmana to combat. Lákshmana, on foot and with only his bow as a weapon, summoned the divine missiles the sage had given to him and Rama when they were young, and cut the demon's head from his glittering body.

The evil news was brought to Rávana by his fleeing soldiers, and he groaned as he heard of the deaths of his sons and the last of his brothers who were faithful to

him. He ordered all the gates to be barricaded, the walls
to be carefully guarded, and a watch kept night and day.
No attack was made, for all his leading warriors were
dead, and he himself despaired of victory. He shut himself in his palace and mourned for those who had died;
and in the grove where she was captive, Sita lifted up her
head and smiled, for Sarama told her of victory after
victory, and day by day she grew less thin and pale in
the hope of seeing Rama.

One son was left to Rávana, the most powerful of all,
Indrajita, who had defeated the God of the Heavens
himself. He found his father sunk in an ocean of grief
and said to him, "Indrajita still lives, dear Father; therefore do not despair! Today you will see Rama and
Lákshmana lying on the earth, torn to pieces by my
arrows that never miss their mark. Give me leave, my
lord, to go forth!"

He trusted completely in his power and in his mastery
of magic that had always brought him victory. When
he had defeated Indra and taken him captive, Brahma
himself, the Creator, with other gods, had come to Lanka
and stood above the city. Rávana and Indrajita came
forth upon the terrace of the palace and Brahma spoke
amiably to them: "Truly your son has borne himself
nobly on the field of battle, O Rávana! He will become
a famous and invincible warrior. Tell us now, what shall
we bestow upon you as ransom for the lord of heaven?"

"Grant me immortality and he shall be set free," answered Indrajita.

"No creature on earth may be immortal, no matter how powerful he is," said Brahma.

"You know, O exalted one, that I worship Agni with daily sacrifice," said Indrajita. "Let his chariot with its horses be at my service whenever I need it, and may I never be struck down while I am mounted upon it! But if I fail in my sacrifice to him, may I perish in battle! Some seek to enter heaven through penance; I wish to enter it through valor."

"Let it be so!" answered Brahma; and Indra returned with the other gods to his abode in the heavens.

Therefore the son of Rávana was certain of victory over Rama, whom he scorned as a mere man. He went forth gaily with a great troop of warriors, to the sound of martial music, but before he reached the battlefield he went aside to a sacred grove and offered his sacrifice to the God of Fire. Then he summoned the chariot of Agni and spoke a magic spell upon himself and all his weapons. He called out to his warriors, "Be of good cheer! Attack the enemy with confidence!" And he himself in his chariot rose from the earth and became invisible.

While the demons fought fiercely, sure of Indrajita's victory, he poured forth a stream of arrows from where he stood and the monkeys could not see whence they came. At first they fled; then remembering their former victories, they returned bravely, throwing rocks and stones in the direction of the deadly arrows. But Indrajita, invisibly ranging the field, overwhelmed that brave army and hundreds of them fell, crying piteously, and

the rest knew not how to save themselves. Then Rávana's son directed his weapons against Rama and
Lákshmana. They, too, sent a shower of arrows into the
air where they thought their enemy must be, but their
shafts fell harmlessly back to earth, while they themselves were targets for Indrajita's skill.

"Let us yield ourselves to these weapons," said Rama to
his brother. "We cannot defeat this master of magic
while he remains invisible. Let him cover us with a rain
of darts! When he sees us lying on the ground, he will
think us dead and will return to Lanka to tell his father
of his great victory."

They defended themselves no longer and soon fell,
unconscious, pierced by the arrows of Indrajita, who
burst into laughter and cried out to his troops, "Behold,
O demons, Rama is dead!" They cheered him wildly,
and in a transport of joy he hastened back to Lanka. He
sought out his father and stood before him with joined
palms, announcing, "Rama and Lákshmana are slain!"
Rávana sprang from his throne, joyfully embraced his
son, and ordered a great celebration in his honor.

Meanwhile Sugriva and Hánuman, who were not
wounded, stood weeping beside the bodies of the two
brothers. But Vibíshana came to them and said, "Have
no fear; they are not dead and will recover. See, the
color has not left their faces. Keep watch over them, O
Sugriva, while Hánuman and I go to encourage and
comfort those who have fallen."

The two of them went all over the battlefield, finding
many dead and many sorely wounded. They came upon

that wise and aged monkey, Jámbavan, whom all respected, and Vibíshana leaned over him to see if he was still alive. In a feeble voice the aged one said, "Tell me, O tiger among demons, does Hánuman still live?"

"He stands here," answered Vibíshana, and Hánuman came forward and touched Jámbavan's feet. "But why do you ask for him instead of the two princes or Sugriva or Angada?"

"Because if he lives, we are all saved," answered Jámbavan, whose voice was stronger since he had seen Hánuman, to whom he now turned. "It is for you to deliver us, O slayer of foes! Cross the great ocean once more and cross the land until you see the peaks of the Himalayas. Then direct your course to `the Golden Mountain, from which you will see the summit of Mt. Kailasa. Between these two rises the peak where all the healing herbs grow. Gather them all, O son of the Storm-God, and come back speedily to help us!"

Hánuman felt himself filled with power; he leaped to the top of a hill and again took in his breath, laid his tail over his back, and sprang into the air, like the discus loosed from the hand of Vishnu. He went farther than he had ever gone before. Under him lay the ocean; then he passed over mountains, rivers, cities, clouds, flights of birds and crowded provinces. Suddenly the Himalayas appeared, the abode of snows, and he beheld the golden peak that Jámbavan had described to him and in the distance the noble summit of Mt. Kailasa. Between them rose the smaller peak of the mountain where the healing herbs grew, and there Hánuman alighted and looked about him. There were a hundred different plants and he did not know which were the right ones; he was in haste to get back and to revive those who lay suffering on the field of battle.

"Why do you not show yourselves to me?" he cried angrily. "Have you no pity for Rama?" And he broke off a great piece of rock on which many plants were growing and sped back over land and sea, carrying it in his arms. He landed with a shout in the monkeys' camp, and they all cried out with joy as they saw him coming. He took the rock to Jámbavan, who picked out the healing herbs, crushed them in his hands and held them to the nostrils of Rama and of Lákshmana. They came at once to their senses and rose to their feet as well and strong as ever. Then all those monkeys who had been struck down by Indrajita were also healed and rose up like sleepers waking in the dawn.

Sugriva was so happy that he called the monkeys together, even though the sun had set. "The demons believe that they have won a victory," he said. "Let us throw ourselves upon the city and set it afire! Light torches!"

With flaming torches in their hands, the monkeys rushed upon the gates, terrifying the sleepy sentinels, who fled away. They entered the city, burning the gates and then the buildings within. Splendid palaces, storehouses, stables, went up in flames, and terrified horses and elephants ran wild through the streets. The shrieks of women and the wailing of children rang through the city. Rávana's warriors had been celebrating Indrajita's victory; they were unarmed and had been feasting and drinking. They picked up their weapons and rushed into the streets and squares, where a frightful battle began, lighted by a waning moon and the flaming buildings. Rama and Lákshmana stood just outside the gates, striking down the enemy with the arrows that never missed their mark, and the demons were terrified to see them, risen, as it seemed, from the dead.

At dawn Rama's army withdrew, but in Lanka Indrajita was furious at his failure and planned a new and surer attack. He set out for the grove outside the city's walls where he always offered his sacrifice to Agni. As he came out of the shattered gate, Vibíshana went to Rama. "Whenever Indrajita goes to battle he offers a sacrifice to Agni," he said. "If he completes that sacrifice he cannot be conquered; Agni also will give him the chariot in which he rides the sky and is invisible. But if he does not complete it he may be slain, for so he vowed in the presence of the gods. He is now in the sacred grove. Send Lákshmana at once, and let him kill that powerful magician before he can complete the rites! When Indrajita is slain, Rávana also is slain."

Lákshmana set out at once with Vibíshana to guide him and an escort of eager monkeys, led by Hánuman. Vibíshana took him to a thick grove in the midst of which stood a great fig tree. There, he said, Indrajita was performing his sacrifice, guarded by his army. "Let your monkeys throw themselves upon these troops and scatter them," said Vibíshana. "Then you will see Indrajita and can fight him."

Lákshmana loosed a flight of arrows against the fiends
and the monkeys tore up trees and rocks and attacked
them fiercely. Hánuman was in fine form and struck
about him so powerfully that the enemy fell back before
him. Indrajita heard the tumult and saw that his forces
were losing; he rose, leaving his sacrifice unfinished; he
summoned the chariot of Agni and mounted it. Lákshmana saw him coming and cried out, "I challenge you
to single combat, O son of Rávana, in a fair fight!"

Indrajita saw Vibíshana standing beside Lákshmana.
"O younger brother of Rávana, why do you try to harm
his son?" he cried scornfully. "You are to be pitied, for
you have no sense of duty or brotherly feeling. Do you
think it wise to leave your own kindred and seek a miserable refuge with strangers? Is it virtuous to abandon your
family and to serve their enemy, O impious wretch?"

"You are proud and ill-mannered, O prince," answered Vibíshana. "You do not know my true nature.
I do not delight in cruelty and anger, in arrogance and
hate, which are my brother's sins. I know that the man
who steals others' wives and does not listen to his friends'
counsel is doomed. You, your father, and Lanka will all
be destroyed. Now enter into combat with Lákshmana
and die!"

Then a great fight took place between those two, Indrajita in his chariot and Lákshmana on foot. They were
both mighty archers and both wore golden mail that no
arrow could pierce. Taunting and insulting one another,
they tried one weapon after another, destroying or parry-
ing the other's arrow while it was in the air. Their move-

ments were so swift that no one could see when they picked up their arrows or let them fly, when they stretched the bowstring or loosed it. They were both wounded and breathed hard, but neither one tired or retreated. Lákshmana knew that his enemy drew added power from the chariot in which he rode; he killed the charioteer, and for a short time Indrajita drove the chariot while he fought, a skillful feat. But four great monkeys threw themselves upon the horses and dragged them to earth, another broke the chariot, and Indrajita was forced to fight on foot.

The two heroes had exhausted their usual weapons; both summoned divine ones that the gods had granted them. They loosed their shafts at once and the two met in the air and burst into flames, like two planets colliding. Then Lákshmana took out his most powerful weapon that had belonged to Indra, god of gods. As he placed it on his great bow, he said to it, "If Rama is truly virtuous and faithful and is the greatest of heroes, then slay this son of Rávana!" He stretched his bowstring to his ear and let fly the weapon, which cut the head of Indrajita from his body. With its diadem and earrings, that splendid head looked like a golden ball thrown on the ground.

All this time the soldiers of both sides had been fighting furiously. But when Indrajita fell, the demons flung down their arms and fled, panic-stricken, in all directions, pursued by the triumphant monkeys. Some reached the gates of the city, others ran up the mountain or threw themselves into the sea. When the monkeys gave up the chase they crowded round Lákshmana, jumping up and down, shouting with joy, clapping their hands, and hugging one another as they praised him. The blessed Indra, who had watched the battle from his dwelling in the heavens, rejoiced at the death of his enemy; the gods struck their gongs and the nymphs scattered flowers upon the victorious warrior.

Then Lákshmana, wounded and leaning on Vibíshana and Hánuman, went back to Rama, who received him in a joyful embrace and listened eagerly as Vibíshana told him all that had happened. "Now that you have slain the conqueror of Indra, O mighty warrior, Rávana himself is defeated," Rama said to his brother. "When he hears of the death of his son, he will come forth and I shall slay him at last. Because of your victory it will not be hard to regain Sita and even the whole earth."

16

The Death of Ravana

When Rávana was told of the death of Indrajita, he
fainted and lay unconscious for a long time, not hearing
the loud lamentation that filled his palace. When he
came to himself, rage filled his heart, fanned by his grief;
flame and smoke came from his mouth and nostrils, and
his tears were like drops of boiling oil falling from two
burning lamps. He started up and said to his warriors
and ministers, "Today I shall take the bow and arrows
given to me by Brahma and destroy both Rama and
Lákshmana. But first I shall slay Sita, the cause of all our
woe!" And he strode from the hall, drawing his great
sword.

His friends held him back, and his wisest minister
stood before him and dared to say, "Why do you give

way to rage, O mighty King, and forget all the laws that
you know so well? You have studied the Vedas: how
can you think of killing a woman? Spare her and turn
your anger upon her lord! This is the last day of the
dark fortnight of the moon; tomorrow, when the new
crescent arises, go forth to victory, and Sita will be yours!"

The unhappy king let himself be led back to the assembly hall and sat upon his throne in a black mood,
breathing like an angry serpent. "Go forth now with all
your strength and hurl yourselves only upon Rama!" he
said to his warriors. "Wound him and wear him out and
tomorrow I shall kill him!"

His warriors summoned all the forces that were left
and assembled all the chariots, elephants, and horses that
could be found in Lanka. They still had confidence in
the power of their king who had never been defeated,
and they fell upon their enemy with fury, trying to cut
a way through their ranks to where Rama and Lákshmana stood ordering the battle and sending showers of
arrows above their soldiers' heads. As they came on,
Rama went down amongst them, shooting his deadly
arrows right and left. Because they were mounted and
he was on foot, they could not see him, and he went
through their ranks as a hurricane passes through a forest, unseen except for the devastation that it leaves.
"There he is!" cried one. "That is he who is destroying
us!" said another, and in their confusion they began to
strike at one another. Finally, their horses slain and
their chariots overturned, those who escaped took refuge
in Lanka.

The next day at dawn Rávana summoned his troops and his own chariot. It blazed with gold and jewels as if it were on fire; it was adorned with rows of bells and filled with darts and spears, bows and quivers, and was drawn by four black horses. Rávana mounted it, his face so furious that none dared to look at him. "Today I shall send Rama and his brother to the abode of Yama, King of the Dead," he said. "When that strong tree falls, Sita, who is its blossom, and all those friends who are its branches, will also fall. I shall avenge my sons and brothers and dry the tears of those who weep for the dead. I shall cover the earth's surface with the bodies of monkeys, and the crows and vultures will be sated with their flesh!"

He rode forth into battle, followed by his troops, and with his divine weapons he scattered the brave monkeys as the wind drives away the clouds, for they could not bear the shafts that had defeated the gods. Amid the dust of battle Rávana drove on to where Rama stood waiting with Lákshmana at his side. "How splendid is this lord of demons!" said Rama to his brother. "One can hardly look upon him, as one cannot look at the sun. Never have I seen such power and brilliance."

Lákshmana wished to be the first to fight and stepped forward, loosing a flight of flaming arrows, but Rávana cut these to pieces with his own shafts. Then he took up a terrible spear, hung with eight loud bells, and hurled it with all his power at Lákshmana, who fell to the ground, struck full in the breast by that great weapon. Rama's heart was stricken as he saw his brother fall, but he thought to himself, "This is not the time for lamentation. Take care of Lákshmana!" he called to the monkeys. "The time for which I have longed has come. Today all my sorrows shall be wiped out when I slay Rávana. Seat yourselves on the mountainside, O unconquerable ones, and watch with peaceful hearts this fight which men will tell about as long as the world lasts!" And he entered fiercely into combat with his foe.

There followed such a struggle as had never been seen on earth, when those two warriors tried to kill one another. Both were skilled archers, both knew all the science of warfare, both had weapons made by the high gods, and neither had ever known defeat. Each sent forth a cloud of arrows as they circled about one another, each had impenetrable armor and stood unwounded. The monkeys gathered in a half circle behind Rama, and the demons stood behind their king, watching one terrific missile after another destroyed or turned aside in midair. Each side shouted with joy as their champion seemed to prevail.

The gods also watched this conflict, for it had been planned by them long ago and on it depended their own safety, their freedom from the wickedness of Rávana, whom they themselves could not kill because of the boon that had been granted him. As they watched, unseen by any on the battlefield, they said to one another, "This is not a fair fight, for Rama is on foot while the demon rides his chariot." Then Indra called to his charioteer, Mátali, "Yoke my chariot quickly and offer it to Rama!"

Mátali harnessed the bay horses, whose coats gleamed

like the sun, and raised the standard of Indra over the beautiful chariot, which he brought to the ground beside Rama. "The lord of a thousand eyes sends this to you so that you may win the victory, O mighty warrior," he said. "Here, too, is the great bow of Indra, his shield and his spear." Rama bowed to the chariot and mounted it, radiant as a god, for he was Vishnu, though he did not know his true nature. Driven by Mátali, that divine charioteer, he assailed Rávana from every side, and that prowler of the night, furious at the favor bestowed on his rival, fought even more fiercely.

He took up a spear as strong as a diamond, hung with loud bells, headed with a spike that flamed and smoked. He lifted it with his powerful arm and cried to Rama, "Now lie beside your brother, O arrogant prince! This lance will end your life." He hurled it, its bells resounding, and Rama flung the lance of Indra, which met the other in the air and shattered it with a sound like thunder.

Then, as he fought, Rama taunted his foe. "What a hero you are, O wicked wretch, to carry off a woman after luring her husband from her by a trick! What a noble deed was that! If I had been there, I would have sent you to join your brother whom I have slain. Now by good fortune you stand before me. Today your head, with its crown and earrings, shall roll in the dust, and vultures will drink the blood that flows from your wounds!" He was so angry that his friends feared to look upon his face, and even Rávana was dismayed. His courage and strength seemed to be redoubled by his rage, and he poured such a rain of arrows on his foe that

Rávana's heart fainted within him and he dropped his bow and sank down on the bench of his chariot.

His driver was troubled by the appearance of the king and turned the black horses, driving them from the field, and Rama, mindful of Kshatria honor, did not pursue his enemy while he was unarmed. Rávana soon came to his senses and spoke angrily, "Are you mad or afraid, O charioteer? Why do you drive me from the field against my orders? Have I no courage or power? Am I a coward or a weakling that you take my fate into your hands and shame me before my enemy? Have you been bribed by him, O villain? Have you no loyalty and no remembrance of the gifts you have received from my hands? Turn back at once before my adversary departs!"

"I am not afraid, nor mad, nor careless, nor unfaithful, nor have I forgotten all your gifts, great King," answered the charioteer calmly. "I saw that you were exhausted by the fight and had dropped your weapons. My horses, too, were tired, like cattle lashed by a storm. It is my duty to watch the expressions and the motions of my master and to judge when to advance and when to retreat, as well as to know where the earth is firm for my wheels and where it is treacherous. It was my devotion to you that made me drive away. Now that you have recovered your confidence, O scourge of your foes, I will do whatever you command."

Rávana took a precious ring from his finger and gave it to his servant. "Drive my chariot quickly back to where Rama stands, O faithful one!" he said. "Rávana never turns back till he has slain his foe."

Meanwhile Rama had time to catch his breath, for he, too, was tired by the dreadful conflict. As he stood on Indra's chariot he was aware of the sun's light pouring down upon him out of a cloudless sky, and he worshiped that god who is the giver of life and victory: "All hail, O creator of life, who nourishes all creatures, who subdues darkness and cold and wickedness! O courser in the heavens, O lord of the stars and planets and worlds, giver of wealth and happiness, O maker of the day, bestower of victory and the joy of victory, I salute you! O golden and brilliant one, the friend of waters, who gathers up the showers from the sea, who creates the seasons, you whose rays behold everything in the three worlds, O you who awaken the lotus, all hail! Bringer of life and death, lord of all actions, I salute you!"

He felt himself filled with new power as he saw the chariot of Rávana bearing down upon him, its black horses at full gallop. He stretched the bow of Indra into the shape of the crescent moon as his skillful driver urged the horses forward and passed Rávana's chariot, covering it with dust. The fearful duel began again, and still neither warrior prevailed, but Rama thought, "I shall win," while Rávana said to himself, "I must die." When it seemed as if every weapon had been exhausted, Rama thought, "These are the same weapons with which I killed Maricha and all the demons in the forest, which pierced the seven trees at Kishkindha and slew Bali. Why is it that they have no power over Rávana?"

Mátali, the wise charioteer, divined his thought and said to him, "Have you forgotten the most powerful one

of all, O lord of men? Loose Brahma's shaft upon him,
for the hour of his doom has come!" Rama summoned
that weapon that was like a winged snake, that hissed
like a viper; he looked upon it with delight and fixed it
on his bow, speaking the incantation. Then with his
whole strength he pulled the bowstring to his ear and
loosed that deadly shaft, which pierced the breast of Rávana and, passing through his body, returned to Rama's
hand. The great fiend, scourge of the three worlds, fell
from his chariot and the earth shook with his fall.

When they saw their lord stretched upon the ground,
his warriors fled, pursued by the victorious monkeys, who
shouted with triumph. Vibíshana and Sugriva, Angada
and Hánuman paid homage to Rama, and Lákshmana,
restored to life by the healing herbs, came and stood beside him with joined palms and a radiant face. Rama
embraced him joyfully, saying, "If I had regained Sita
and my kingdom and even the whole world, they would
be as nothing to me if I had lost you." As they stood
there in the joy of victory and the army returned from
its pursuit and crowded around, acclaiming Rama,
flowers fell upon them from the sky, and all about them
resounded the music of the gods and the throbbing of
celestial drums.

The monkeys went to gaze upon the great body of Rávana and looked with awe at his mighty arms and weapons. He was mortally wounded but still breathing. Rama
and Lákshmana drew near and the monkeys made way
for them. "You have been a mighty warrior and a great
king, O Rávana," said Rama. "You have lived for a thou-

sand years and traversed the three worlds. What counsel can you give me, O mighty one?"

"You are no mortal man, O Rama," answered the dying fiend, gasping for his breath. "No mortal could have slain me. I salute you! This is my counsel: if you wish to do a good deed, do it at once; but if you plan an evil deed, think carefully before doing it!" His breath failed him and he suffered from his wound. "Once I was sorry for all those creatures who longed to go to the dwelling of the gods and found it so hard to reach. I wished to have a stairway built by the gods' own architect from earth to heaven to make the journey easier. Each day I put it off, and it was never done. But when my sister came to me and told me of the death of Khara in the forest and the beauty of Sita, I resolved to steal her away and did so at once. Thus I brought about my death." His body shuddered and he yielded up his life.

Vibíshana came and stood beside Rama. He looked at his brother's body and remembered his former greatness, his generosity to his friends and kinsmen, and their long life together; he began to lament for him, with tears, but Rama said, "No one should mourn a warrior slain in battle. He had great courage and fell without yielding; he met a Kshatria's death. Now with all honor perform his funeral rites."

Then Vibíshana remembered his brother's sins and said, "How can I honor one who failed to fulfill his vows, who was ruthless and cruel, who killed holy sages and stole the wives of others? He deserves no honor."

"Death ends all enmity," answered Rama. "This

prowler of the night was always brave, though he was wicked. We have accomplished our purpose; he is no longer our enemy. It is right for me as well as for you to perform his funeral rites, for he is your brother and therefore mine."

Vibíshana returned to Lanka and came back followed by a crowd of citizens and many carts carrying all that was needed for the ceremony. They built a great pyre and covered it with rich cloths and garlands and perfumes and laid upon it the body of their king. All his queens came forth with weeping and lamentation; all his ministers and the chief citizens of Lanka came and took their places according to their ages and honors. The sacred rites were performed, and Vibíshana kindled the flame. When the pyre was consumed to ashes, the weeping women returned to their homes.

Then Rama turned to his brother and said, "Now let us make Vibíshana the King of Lanka!" Lákshmana sent monkeys to the ocean to bring its water for the ceremony and ordered others to raise a high seat on the battlefield, and there, according to the sacred rites, Vibíshana was crowned the king of all the demons. The counselors and citizens paid homage to him with great joy, for they loved and honored him.

When these two ceremonies were accomplished, Rama turned to Hánuman. "Now enter the city, O my friend," he said, "and find Sita. Tell her that Rávana is dead and that Lákshmana and I are well. Give her these good tidings, O prince of monkeys, and ask her what she wishes to do!"

17

Sita's Ordeal

Hánuman entered Lanka by its principal gate, and all the citizens bowed down before him. He went through the great palace, filled with the wailing of women, to the grove where he had found Sita weeks before. She was still there, surrounded by her guards, and she looked up joyfully as she saw him bowing before her, his joined hands touching his brow.

"O noble princess, Rama and Lákshmana are well and greet you," he said. "Rávana is dead and Vibíshana is King of Lanka. So you need have no more fear or anxiety, O virtuous one!" Sita's face became as radiant as the full moon, but she could find no words to express her joy. "What are you thinking, O goddess," asked Hánuman, "since you do not answer me?"

"For a moment I could not speak for joy," said Sita, her voice trembling. "O prince of monkeys, what can I offer you in return for this happy news? Gold or jewels or even a throne could not equal this message of yours. You have strength and courage, boldness and endurance, faithfulness and humility, O Hánuman, my son!"

"I ask one boon of you," said Hánuman. "Allow me to slay these evil women who have treated you so roughly and spoken such ugly words to you. I wish to beat them with my fists, tear them to pieces with my teeth, chew up their ears and noses, pull out their hair, and then kill them, dear Mother, because they have caused you pain."

Sita laughed at him and said, "Who can be angry with servants who merely obey their lord's command, O lion among apes? If Rávana is dead they can no longer torment me. There is an old and wise saying; listen to it, O Hánuman! We should never return evil for evil, but have compassion upon the wicked even while they are injuring us."

"You are worthy of Rama," said Hánuman humbly. "Now tell me what you desire, O lovely one, for he awaits your message."

"I wish to see my lord," answered Sita simply.

"You shall see him today, with Lákshmana and all his devoted friends," said Hánuman.

He returned directly to Rama, told him how Sita looked and gave him her message. Rama sighed deeply, then turned to Vibíshana and said, "Bring the daughter of Jánaka hither, I pray you, after she has bathed and dressed and adorned herself."

When Vibíshana gave her this message, bowing low before her, Sita said, "I wish to see my lord at once, O King of Lanka, just as I am." But the newly crowned king, splendid in his royal robes, said gently, "A noble queen should do what her lord desires, O Sita."

He led her into the palace where his wife, Sita's good friend, and her ladies welcomed her. They took off the dusty garment she had worn so long, bathed her, and rubbed her body with perfumed ointments. They washed her beautiful hair, dried it over fragrant fires and brushed it until it was soft and shining again. Then they dressed her in a robe of finest silk and hung jewels about her neck, on her ears, about her ankles and wrists, and put a garland of fresh flowers on her hair. With her radiant face, she looked as beautiful as a goddess.

Vibíshana was waiting for her with a curtained litter borne on the shoulders of four attendants and followed by an escort of the palace guards. The citizens filled the streets, trying to see this woman for whom Rávana had been slain and their proud city conquered. When the litter passed through the gates and approached the camp, the monkeys and demons also crowded around it, peering through the curtains at this princess for whom so many had lost their lives. Vibíshana went ahead and said joyfully to Rama, who was standing absorbed in his own thoughts, "She is coming!"

When Rama heard that his beloved wife, who had lived so long in Rávana's palace, was coming to him, his heart was filled with joy and anger and sorrow. He said to Vibíshana, "Bring her nearer to me, my friend!" Vibí-

shana wished to clear the way for the litter and ordered
the demons who escorted Sita to drive away all those
who crowded around it trying to see her. The guards began to lay about them with their staves, and an uproar
arose as the monkeys were pushed back. "Why do you
drive them away?" said Rama angrily to Vibíshana.
"Are they not my people? I look upon them all as if they
were my own family; have they not a right to see their
queen? In times of danger, at her bridal choice, and at
her marriage a woman may be seen unveiled. Let Sita
come hither on foot, so that all may see her!" Everyone
was astonished at his voice and his face, which was
clouded, his eyebrows drawn together in a frown.

Sita stepped from the litter and found herself in the
midst of a great crowd of strangers who gazed at her,
amazed at her grace and beauty. She had never faced so
many people before and shrank within herself for a moment; then she saw her dearly loved husband and forgot
everything else. Standing before him with tears of joy in
her eyes, she could only say, "My lord!" Then, when
he did not answer but stayed with downcast eyes, her joy
was chilled by fear. This was not the meeting she had
longed for during her year of suffering, and she did not
understand. She controlled her tears, summoned all her
courage, and stood, with the dignity of a pure conscience,
awaiting her husband's pleasure.

Rama looked up at last and spoke. "I have regained
you, O noble lady, and my enemy is dead; my wrath is
quenched, for the evil deed and the doer of it have both
been wiped out by my prowess. All my efforts have been

crowned with success; I have fulfilled my vow and am free. Hánuman, too, plucks the fruit of his courage; Sugriva and Vibíshana reap the harvest of their labors and their valor."

While he spoke Sita looked at him, her beautiful eyes wide with surprise and filled with tears. Seeing her so close to him, Rama's anguish increased, but he spoke cruelly to her. "Do not think, O daughter of Jánaka, that this difficult war was won entirely for your sake. I cherish my honor and have slain Rávana in order to avenge the insult offered to my noble family. Now go where you please, for I can have nothing more to do with you. What man, what king, could take back a wife who has dwelt for a year in another's house? Rávana's wicked eyes have rested upon you and he has held you in his arms. Therefore go, O lovely one, wherever you desire! Lákshmana or Bhárata, Vibíshana or Sugriva will protect and care for you; you may choose between them!"

Sita had never before heard an unkind word from him. These cruel and insulting words, spoken before that multitude, pierced her heart as if they were sharp arrows. She hid her face and wept bitterly; then she raised her head, wiped her eyes and answered proudly.

"Why do you speak thus, my lord, as if I were a worthless woman? Am I still a stranger to you, despite all the years of our life together? If my body was touched by Rávana as he carried me away, it was against my will. What could I do? My heart has always been yours. When you sent Hánuman to find me, why did you not renounce me then? I should have yielded up my life in his presence, O mighty hero, and you need not have wearied yourself and your friends in battle or lost any lives for my sake. I am called the daughter of Jánaka though I am truly born of the goddess Earth; I am worthy of your respect, not of your scorn. How can you misjudge me so; how can you forget the joining of our hands in marriage and our vows? You have given way to anger and suspicion and acted ignobly, O lion among men!"

She turned to Lákshmana, who was overcome with sorrow, and said to him, "Build a pyre for me, O Láksh-mana, my brother. There is only one way left for me to go, since I have been renounced here in this assembly by my husband. I cannot bear any more."

Lákshmana looked at his elder brother and saw by his expression that Rama did not forbid him. Therefore he ordered the monkeys to bring wood, and he built the pyre while all of Rama's friends and all who were present looked on, silent and stricken, none daring to appeal to him or even to look at him.

Lákshmana kindled the fire, and Sita, her hands joined, walked around Rama three times, keeping him on her right. Then she approached the blazing pile. She made obeisance to all the gods, with joined palms, and then spoke to Agni, God of Fire: "O you who live within the bodies of all living creatures and know their inmost being, if I have always been true to Rama, protect me! If I have been pure in thought and deed, O Agni, you who witness all things, save and protect me!"

With these words she walked fearlessly into the flames, and a terrible cry of fear and sorrow rose from all those

who watched her. She was like gold cast into the cruci-
ble, like a sacrificial victim given to the fire.

Then all the gods hastened to that place in their chariots bright as the sun. Led by Indra of the thousand eyes
they gathered around and above that multitude: Yama,
king of the Dead, Varuna, God of the Waters, and
Vayu, God of the Wind; Kúvera, the God of Wealth,
the older brother of Rávana and Vibíshana, came back
to the city that had once been his; and with them came
the high gods: Shiva the Destroyer, the three-eyed one
who rides the bull; and Brahma who created the worlds.

In their presence Agni, God of Fire, stilled the flames
upon the pyre and came forth from it, leading Sita by
the hand. She was more beautiful than when she entered
the fire, for now her face was radiant with joy and she
smiled; not a hair of her lovely head or a thread of her
robes was singed, nor a jewel cracked.

Agni put her hand in Rama's and said, "Here is your
noble wife, O Rama; there is no fault in her. She has
never been unfaithful to you in thought, in deed, in
speech, or even in the glance of an eye. Imprisoned, alone,
threatened and tempted, she thought only of you. I see
all that is visible and all that is hidden; her heart is
known to me. Receive her and cherish her!"

Rama's face was as joyful as Sita's as he took her in
his arms. "It was necessary for Sita to pass through this
trial, for she had dwelt for a long time in Rávana's palace," he said. "Otherwise the people would have questioned her honor and mine. I have always known that
she was true to me. Rávana could no more have come

near to her, even in thought, than he could have put his hand into a flame. I could never renounce her, for she is to me as the light is to the sun, as his valor is to a warrior."

So at last, after all their suffering, they were united in great joy, while Lákshmana, Vibíshana, and all those who saw these wondrous things rejoiced and were comforted.

Then Indra spoke to Rama, saying, "It is well for all beings that you have accomplished this great feat, O best of men, and rid the three worlds of the dread of Rávana. Go now and rule over Ayodhya! Console your pure and devoted wife and seek out your brother Bhárata and bring joy to your mothers! We are all greatly pleased with you; therefore ask any boon that you desire, O scourge of your foes!"

"If you wish to please me, O chief of the gods," answered Rama, who held Sita close to his side, "let all those brave monkeys who left their homes and died for my sake be brought back to life! May they rise up with no pain or wounds, in all their strength and joy, and be reunited with their families! And let there be flowers and fruits, honey and pure water wherever they may go!"

"This boon is hard to grant, O mighty hero, but I shall keep my word and do as you desire," said Indra.

And all those monkeys who lay dead, with severed heads and limbs, rose up, healed, as if they had been asleep, and looked at one another, asking, "Where are we?" "Where are all our enemies?" "Let us kill them!" Then they saw that the victory had been won and they embraced one another; they met all their friends and surrounded Rama, acclaiming him.

The gods themselves made obeisance to Rama and then returned joyfully to the celestial regions. Rama bade a grateful farewell to Mátali, the divine charioteer, who had helped him in the battle; and Mátali yoked the bay horses, which leaped into the sky and in a flash bore him out of sight. Then that great company of happy people rested in the joy of victory, sleeping blissfully in their encampment; for Rama still kept his hermit's vow and would not enter Lanka.

18

The Return to Ayodhya

The next morning Vibíshana came to Rama and said, "Your exile is over, O King of Koshala. Will you not bathe and anoint yourself and put on royal raiment? My servants, skilled in the care and dress of the body, attend you."

"Let the leaders of the forest folk be bathed and dressed, O King," said Rama. "I wish to return to Ayodhya, for my faithful brother Bhárata suffers on my account. I pray you, let us return at once, for the way is long and arduous."

"You can return to Ayodhya in one day, O best of men!" said Vibíshana. "Rávana took from our eldest brother a chariot that flies through the air with the speed of thought; it was made by the god who built Lanka

228

and is as bright as a cloud. But I beg of you, if you have any love for me, to stay here for just one day and to accept the honors and the hospitality that I have prepared for you and your friends and all your valiant army."

"Do not be angry, O my friend, if I cannot grant your request," answered Rama. "My heart compels me to see Bhárata, who came to the forest to offer me the kingdom and whom I refused. I long to see my mothers, my house, the people of Ayodhya, and my country. Give me leave, O Vibíshana, and prepare that chariot at once so that we may depart!"

Vibíshana brought the wonderful car which was like a king's palace, with many charming rooms gilded and adorned with jewels, seats covered with rich stuffs, and wide windows. It was hung with bells that gave sweet music and was drawn by white swans. When he had brought it, Vibíshana bowed before Rama and asked, "What more can I do, O King of men?"

"These rangers of the woods have brought about my victory and given you your kingdom, O lord of Lanka," said Rama. "They did not fear to lose their lives and did not yield in battle. Reward them, O King, as I cannot do, since I have no possessions." Vibíshana took the monkeys into the city and into the palace, where he opened the treasury and gave to all of them jewels and gold and fine raiment. Soon they came leaping and rejoicing out of the battered gates to show their wealth to Rama.

Then Rama mounted the chariot, with Lákshmana beside him and Sita held close to his breast, and he bade

them all farewell with love and gratitude. But Sugriva
and Vibíshana and a clamor of voices from the monkeys
cried out, "Take us all with you to Ayodhya, O Rama!
We wish to see you crowned and to pay homage to the
noble Bhárata and your mothers. Then we shall hasten
back to our homes, O King of men!"

"Nothing could give me more pleasure," answered
Rama. "Take your places quickly, O Sugriva, with your
counselors, and you, O Vibíshana, with yours." That divine chariot, drawn by its white swans, rose swiftly into
the air at Rama's command, carrying them all. Rama,
with Sita beside him, looked down on the scenes of his
search and his battle.

"Look, beloved, at the battlefield where so many died
for your sake," he said. "There Hánuman slew a great
brother of Rávana's; in that grove Lákshmana killed Indrajita, who had defeated the lord of heaven. On this
field the other sons of Rávana died, struck down by
brave monkeys. And there Rávana was slain by me for
the wrong he did you. Here we crossed the ocean and
spent the first night. Behold the bridge, O lovely one,
built by Nala over the restless waves of ocean; there, on
the northern shore, was our headquarters while it was
built. That is where Vibíshana came to us. O Sita, behold
Kishkindha, Sugriva's city, where I slew his brother Bali.
Beside it is the cave where Lákshmana and I spent the
weary months of the rains, where I should have died of
despair without his cheer and courage."

"I wish that Sugriva's queen and all the wives of our
friends could come to Ayodhya with us," said Sita shyly.

Rama caused the chariot to halt, and it came down gently in front of the great city hollowed out of the rock. Sugriva went to his palace and ordered his queens and the wives of his counselors to adorn themselves hastily and to follow him. They came out, eager to behold Sita, who received them graciously, and the chariot rose again and sped on.

Rama looked down again on that vast country through which he and Lákshmana had traveled on foot, anxious and sorrowful, over which Sita had been carried, crying out in despair, by Rávana. "On that great mountain I first met Sugriva, O Sita, and made the alliance with him," he said. "It is there that you dropped your jewels, O beautiful one, and he picked them up. Do you see that lovely lake? We were there in the spring, and I wept for you because you loved that season so dearly. And there is our hermitage in the clearing of the forest. Now I can see Chitrakuta, where Bhárata came to beg me to return. Behold the shining Jumna and the holy Ganges and the retreat of that sage who gave us shelter! Ah Lákshmana, there is our own river and, far off, are the walls and towers of our father's city. Bow down to Ayodhya, O daughter of Jánaka; we have come home at last!"

He did not go to Ayodhya, however, but turned the chariot back to the hermitage of the sage who had welcomed them in the first days of their exile. There they all descended, and Rama bowed before the holy one and asked him, "Are all well and happy in the city, O blessed one? Are my mothers still living? Does Bhárata always tread the path of duty?"

"Bhárata rules the kingdom wisely, in hermit's garb, with your sandals on the throne beside him, my son," said the sage. "Your mothers are well and all long for your return. Now, O victorious one, stay here and refresh yourselves; enter Ayodhya tomorrow and ask of me whatever boon you desire."

"I ask this boon of you, O fount of wisdom," answered Rama, bowing his head. "Let all the trees bear honeyed fruit in abundance, even though their season is past, for these friends of mine!"

The boon was granted immediately, and the monkeys thought themselves in heaven as they fell upon those fruitful, blossoming trees that fairly dripped with honey, while Rama and Sita, Lákshmana and Vibíshana sat with the sage and shared his frugal meal. Because of his holy life he knew all that had befallen them and all that had happened in Ayodhya, and they listened eagerly to him, for they had had no news of all those whom they loved since Bhárata left them fourteen years ago.

While it was still day, Rama took Hánuman aside and said to him, "Go with all speed to Ayodhya, O best of monkeys! On the way, seek out Guha, who dwells by the Ganges; salute him in my name and tell him that we are safe and well. He will be glad, for he is my friend. Then go to Bhárata in Nandigrama, where he dwells, and tell him all that has happened and that I am returning with Sugriva and Vibíshana. Notice carefully, my friend, Bhárata's expression, his gestures, and his looks; they will tell you how he receives the news. Who would not be tempted by an ancestral throne and a rich kingdom? I know his heart; he is without fault and would give his life for me; yet, if he shows by the slightest sign that he wishes to keep the kingdom, it shall be his and he shall reign over it for many happy years. When you know his thought, return to me before we have gone farther."

Hánuman took on a human form, since he was meeting strangers who might understand him more easily in that guise. He traveled by the path of the wind and stopped at the bank of the Ganges to give Guha the happy news of Rama's return. Flying on, he saw the towers and the gates of Ayodhya, but another city lay between him and the capital, and this one he took to be Nandigrama, where Bhárata lived and held his court. Many people had gathered about him there, and the village had grown into a large town, handsome and prosperous. It was not hard for Hánuman to mingle with the crowd and to discover the dwelling of Bhárata. He found the king sitting at the entrance of a small hermitage, dressed in deerskins, his hair knotted on his head, as Rama's was.

Hánuman bowed to him, his joined hands at his brow, and said, "I bring you good news, O King. Your brother Rama, for whom you grieve, salutes you and asks if you are well. He is returning from exile, his purpose accomplished. The mighty Lákshmana and the illustrious Sita, his devoted companions, are coming with him and you shall soon behold them."

Bhárata fainted with the sudden joy of this news. He recovered immediately, rose up and embraced Hánuman with tears of happiness. "Are you a man or a god, O my friend, who come to me with such good tidings?" he asked. "Accept from me a hundred cows, a hundred prosperous villages, a hundred lovely serving maidens, skilled in all the arts, and anything else you may desire that I can give you! What joy you have brought to me! All my longings are satisfied, for I shall see Rama again. Now tell me all that has befallen him since I left him in the forest fourteen years ago!"

Hánuman told him the whole story, ending with the words, "He is spending this night in the hermitage of the sage who dwells at the meeting place of the Ganges and the Jumna. You may behold him at sunrise tomorrow, O wise prince, when all the stars will be favorable." Then Hánuman sped back to Rama to tell him that Bhárata, overcome with joy, was preparing to welcome him the next day.

Meanwhile Bhárata called his brother Shátrughna, who rejoiced with him, and they planned for the morrow. Shátrughna summoned workmen together and ordered them to widen and sweep the road between Nandigrama and Ayodhya, to sprinkle it with water and flowers, and to set up banners along the main highways of the capital. Bhárata sent heralds to announce in the public squares, "Let all righteous men purify themselves and worship the gods and the sacred altars of the city with fragrant garlands and music. Let the queens, the ministers, the army, the court, the Brahmans, and the foremost merchants and artisans of the city, led by bards and musicians, form into companies at dawn tomorrow; for

Rama is returning and we shall all go forth to meet him." The news flew from street to street, from house to house, "Rama is coming! Rama is coming!"

Everyone poured out of the houses, the shops, and the markets, chattering and laughing and asking questions. Those who had watched Rama's departure with so much sorrow thanked the gods that they were alive to see him return. Children who had never seen him asked a hundred questions, and the story of his banishment to keep his father's word, the faithfulness of Sita and of Lákshmana, was told again and again. Then everyone was busy decorating both Nandigrama and Ayodhya and no one slept that night. While it was yet light, flowers were gathered from every garden and woven into garlands; flags were hung from every house; perfumes were prepared to sprinkle the streets, and pots of incense were set up, to be lighted at dawn. Sweetmeats and cooling drinks were made ready, and in the royal palaces cooks and servingmen and women, dancers and musicians, armorers and stablemen worked in a fever of joy and excitement to make everything ready. Many of them remembered how they had prepared for Rama's coronation so many years before; now they were sure that no evil thing could happen.

When dawn came the company set forth, some on foot, some on elephants, some in chariots or on horseback; the queens and all the ladies of the court rode in their litters, led by Kaushalya, Rama's mother, and Sumitra, the mother of Lákshmana. All marched in orderly groups, as Bhárata had commanded, and he led them with

Shátrughna, both of them clad in rough cloth and deer-skins. Bhárata bore the sandals of Rama, and Shátrughna held over them the royal canopy, white as the moon, and carried the white yaks' tails with golden handles. Drums and gongs beat, conch shells blared above the noise of hoofs and wheels, and the earth trembled as the city went forth to meet Rama.

When they had gone a short way Bhárata looked at Hánuman, who had returned and walked near him in a man's shape. "You told me that we should behold Rama at sunrise," said Bhárata. "Have you indulged your monkey nature and played a trick on us, O friend?"

"I fear that it is the monkeys that have delayed his coming," answered Hánuman, somewhat abashed, "for I see a great cloud of dust over the woods by the river and I hear their shouts of joy. The holy sages gave them a boon, at Rama's request, that all the trees should bear fruits and honey, and they are surely shaking those trees and plundering them. But behold, O noble prince, there is the chariot of Rama, bright as the moon, glittering in the sunlight, rising above the trees!"

A shout arose from all that crowd of people, "He is come!" And they alighted from their vehicles, horses and elephants, and all pressed forward on foot as the chariot came to earth and they saw Rama standing within it, looking as radiant as Indra.

Bhárata entered the chariot and prostrated himself at the feet of Rama, who raised him and held him close in his arms. Then he reverently saluted Sita and embraced Lákshmana, and Shátrughna followed him and greeted them all with joy. Bhárata had heard from Hánuman all that Sugriva and his army of monkeys had done; he clasped each one of them in his arms and said to Sugriva, "We are four brothers; you shall be the fifth, O ranger of the woods." And to Vibíshana he said, "May you be blessed! Because of your help, a mighty deed was done."

Rama left his chariot and went to his mother's litter, where he knelt and touched her feet, while she gazed upon him, weeping with joy. Sumitra welcomed her son, and both queens took Sita to their hearts. Kaikeyi remained in her curtained litter and thought bitterly to herself, "If Rama comes to me and calls me 'Mother' as he used to do, then I shall live; if he does not, I shall take this poison"; for she had brought a small vial of poison with her. Rama came to her and parted the curtains, bowing to her feet. "I have come home at last, Mother," he said. "Do not grieve; it was destiny, the will of the gods, that caused all our sorrow, and much good has come of it."

"Destiny has treated me cruelly, for it made me speak words that I never wished to speak," answered Kaikeyi, "and I shall always be hated because of them. But truly, in my heart, O Rama, I loved you even better than I loved Bhárata."

Rama paid obeisance to the high priest and greeted all the citizens, who stood with joined hands and acclaimed him, crying, "All hail! Welcome, O protector of the worlds!" Their hands raised in greeting made them look like a great lake covered with lotuses.

Then Bhárata asked his elder brother to be seated

again in the chariot. He brought the sandals and, kneeling, placed them on Rama's feet, saying to him, "The kingdom that you entrusted to me I now return to you. The purpose of my life and all my desires are fulfilled now that you have come back to reign in Ayodhya. Examine, O King, your treasury, your storehouses, and your granaries; for your sake I have increased them tenfold." There were tears in the eyes of Vibíshana and the monkeys as they heard these noble words, and Rama embraced his brother again and seated him at his side, holding him close. Then, followed by the ministers and all the people, they went on to Nandigrama. When they arrived there, Rama dismissed the glorious chariot, saying to it, "Now go and serve your rightful owner, the God of Wealth, who lives in the northern mountains." And that brilliant vehicle rose like a bubble into the air and vanished in the northern sky.

Shátrughna summoned barbers and other servants, and the four brothers bathed; their knotted hair was cut and washed and brushed with fragrant oils; their bodies, too, were rubbed by skillful attendants and anointed with attar of roses and sandalwood powder. Bhárata brought the royal robes and jewels and put them on his elder brother, while Shátrughna brought fine raiment for his twin, Lákshmana. What eager and joyful talk there was among the brothers, as Bhárata and Shátrughna listened to the story of Sita's abduction, the campaign against Lanka, and the victory, for Hánuman had told it briefly! Rama and Lákshmana, also, had much to hear from the two who had so faithfully ruled the kingdom.

Rama and Sita in the Divine Chariot

In another palace the three queens bathed and dressed Sita and heard her story with deep sympathy and love, praising her bravery and her steadfastness. They also dressed the wives of the monkey leaders in lovely garments and jewels, and those charming creatures thought themselves in heaven.

When all was done, Bhárata said to Rama, "Let all the world behold your coronation tomorrow at sunrise, O lord of earth! We have been too long without a master. Henceforth you shall wake and fall asleep to the sound of sweet music and the tinkling of anklets and of girdles. May you rule the world as long as the sun rises and sets and the earth endures!"

"So be it!" answered Rama.

Sumantra, that faithful minister who had driven Rama away from the city on the day of his exile, brought the royal chariot to Nandigrama and Rama seated himself in it. Bhárata took the reins, Shátrughna held the shining canopy and Lákshmana the fan, while Sugriva and Vibíshana stood behind that lord of earth, waving the snow-white yaks' tails over his head. Behind him Hánuman, Angada, and the other monkey leaders, splendidly attired, rode on great elephants; and then came the litters, carried on men's shoulders, that bore Sita and the queens and the ladies of Sugriva's court.

The people of Nandigrama streamed after the procession, and the people of Ayodhya came forth to meet it. Ah, what joy there was in that city when Rama appeared, sitting among his brothers like the moon among the stars, all of them clad again in princely garments and as beautiful as gods! That royal city had not had a king for fourteen years, for Bhárata and Shátrughna had kept their hermit's vows and had never entered it. Now it was one great festival; every house was decorated, flags waved in the bright sun, incense rose from great pots, and the streets were crowded with happy people raising their hands in salutation and praising Rama and Sita and his brothers. Musicians and poets walked before him, drums and cymbals resounded.

They came to the royal palace and entered it, where all was ready for them. Sugriva, Vibíshana, and Hánuman were given splendid palaces, and all the monkeys were entertained with great honor, for Rama had told his ministers what they had done and that he could never have regained Sita and taken Lanka without their help and Vibíshana's.

Preparations were made for the coronation, which was to be at dawn the next day. Sugriva said to Shátrughna, "Water should be brought from all the oceans to consecrate this lord of earth. My valiant monkeys can bring it if you give them leave, O noble prince." Shátrughna gave him four golden urns, and Sugriva called the four most powerful of his leaders, sending each one in a different direction, and giving the hardest task to Hánuman, who was to bring the water of the icy northern sea. They all returned before dawn, their urns filled, and the ceremony began, led by the high priest and the chief Brahmans.

Rama was seated on the royal throne and beside him

was Sita, his equal in beauty and majesty. His brothers stood on each side, and in the hall the Brahmans, the chief warriors, and merchants witnessed the rites. The high priest consecrated him with the pure waters of the oceans, placed the crown of his ancestors on his head and the royal robe on his shoulders.

It is said that the gods themselves came to the palace; that Vayu, the Wind-God, gave Rama a garland made of golden lotuses, and that Indra, God of Heaven, gave him a necklace of shining jewels. The heavenly musicians sang and struck their instruments, and the nymphs themselves danced there in honor of Rama. The earth also gave forth rich crops; trees and flowers blossomed and yielded their fragrance whether or not it was their season.

Rama gave to Sugriva a golden crown set with precious stones, and two bracelets inlaid with emeralds to Angada. He had given to Sita a necklace of pearls that shone like moonbeams, set with other precious gems. Now she unclasped it from her neck, looking first at those handsome monkeys and then at her lord. Rama understood her and said, "Give it to that warrior who pleases you most, O lovely one, whom you find most courageous, strong, and true." She took it off and placed it round the neck of Hánuman, and that lion among monkeys looked splendid, like a mountain ringed with moonlit clouds. Rama gave hundreds and thousands of cows and horses and much gold to the Brahmans of his realm, and richly rewarded all his friends.

When all the festivities were over, Vibíshana and his

counselors returned to Lanka to reign over it justly, harming no creature in the three worlds. Sugriva and his followers took their leave also and returned to Kishkindha, overwhelmed with honors. When Hánuman came to say farewell, Rama said to him, "I have not rewarded you fittingly, O prince of monkeys, for there is no gift that could equal all that you have done for me. Ask for a boon, then, for I will grant you anything in my power."

"I wish to live as long as your name is spoken on earth, O King of men," answered Hánuman.

"So be it!" said Rama. "May you be blessed! You shall live, never ill, never growing old, as long as the earth turns!"

Sita added her boon, "May the gods honor you as an immortal and the celestial nymphs sing and dance for you whenever you desire, O sinless one!" she said. "Wherever you are, may pure streams and luscious fruits appear for love of you!"

Hánuman touched Rama's feet with his forehead and bowed low before Sita, then took his leave sorrowfully and returned with his companions to Kishkindha.

He must be living still in the forests of India; sometimes he may appear in towns and cities, as a simple monkey, to hear the name of Rama spoken and his story told or acted out, as it is every year; sometimes he may watch the athletes as they run and jump and wrestle, for he is the god of all such sports; or visit the many shrines and temples where his image stands and where he is worshiped for his courage, his love and his faithfulness.

Rama reigned over the earth for many happy years. Bhárata was his heir and always at his right hand; Lákshmana and Shátrughna were his ministers and the leaders of his armies. He offered the great sacrifices to the gods many times: the Horse Sacrifice and the Rajasuya, for the kings of all the surrounding countries accepted his dominion and gladly paid tribute to him. In the safety of Ayodhya, Sita bore twin sons, and all the brothers had sons to carry on the noble line of Koshala.

There was no danger of disease or of snakebite during his reign; no woman lacked a husband; men lived long and no parent lost a child. There was no robbery or violence, for men forgot their enmity when they looked at Rama or remembered his deeds. Each man performed his own work and all prospered, for trade flourished in a land where peace and justice prevailed. Skilled artisans came to its cities; scholars and learned Brahmans came to Ayodhya and blessed it. Rain fell as it was needed and was held by dams and in reservoirs for use in the dry season. Crops and fruits were plentiful, and herds of sleek, round cattle and horses filled the pastures.

Indeed, if men speak of happiness or look forward to a time when peace and plenty prevail in the world, they say, "May it be like the reign of Rama!"

This is the story composed by the blessed sage Valmiki. He who hears it constantly is freed from misfortune; he who masters his anger and listens to it with faith overcomes all obstacles: he will return safely from journeys to foreign lands and will rejoice the hearts of his family; he will obtain all his desires and success in all his undertakings; women who hear it will give birth to noble and famous sons, even as Kaushalya gave birth to Rama, Sumitra to Lákshmana and Shátrughna, and Kaikeyi to Bhárata. The hearing of it brings prosperous families, wealth and grain in abundance, lovely wives, brotherly love, wisdom, long life, and peace to those houses where it is known.

Rama is ever pleased with those who listen to this story or who tell the whole of it, and those who do so will attain happiness like unto that of Rama, he whose deeds are imperishable, he who is Vishnu, the Eternal, the Lord.

May prosperity attend you! Recite it with love and may the power of Vishnu increase!

About the Author

ELIZABETH SEEGER's version of the other great Indian epic, *The Mahabhárata,* was published by William R. Scott in 1967. Called *The Five Sons of King Pandu,* it was widely acclaimed by reviewers and selected as one of the best books of the year by the editors of *School Library Journal.*

Miss Seeger, a teacher of history and literature for many years at the Dalton School in New York City, is also author of *Pageant of Chinese History* and *Pageant of Russian History,* both published by David McKay & Co. Miss Seeger lives in Bridgewater, Connecticut.

About the Artist

GORDON LAITE's magnificent illustrations for *The Five Sons of King Pandu* won him awards from *The Society of Illustrators* and *The American Institute of Graphic Arts.* A distinguished artist, Mr. Laite has had numerous one-man shows of his work.

Mr. Laite has long maintained an interest in Oriental culture and is a member of the Bahá'í Faith, which originated in Persia and whose theme revolves around the oneness of man.

Mr. and Mrs. Laite and their daughter are residents of Honduras.